Lindsay Sutton

111 Places in Lancaster & Morecambe That You Shouldn't Miss

Photographs by David Taylor

T0346664

emons:

© Emons Verlag GmbH
All rights reserved
© Photographs by David Taylor, except:
Royal Kings Arms (ch. 80): Ginny Koppenhol
(courtesy of the Royal Kings Arms Hotel)
Layout: Eva Kraskes, based on a design
by Lübbeke | Naumann | Thoben
Maps: altancicek.design, www.altancicek.de
Basic cartographical information from Openstreetmap,
© OpenStreetMap-Mitwirkende, OdbL
Editing: Martin Sketchley
Printing and binding: Grafisches Centrum Cuno, Calbe
Printed in Germany 2022
ISBN 978-3-7408-1557-8
First edition

Guidebooks for Locals & Experienced Travelers
Join us in uncovering new places around the world at
www.111places.com

Foreword

Morecambe Bay got into my blood many years ago. After completing a cross-bay walk, I became a voluntary assistant to the Queen's Guide to the Sands, helping thousands of charity walkers cross the often-treacherous shifting sands and changing channels. From there, I rediscovered Morecambe, then Lancaster, and all the surrounding places where I carved out my career as a newspaper reporter. My book, *Sands of Time*, was the result, and this book has followed. Although my career took on a national and international dimension, this part of Lancashire remains special.

As a writer, you seek the unusual, off-beat and quirky: the routine and the mundane just will not do. Everyone knows that Eric Bartholomew changed his surname to Morecambe, after his hometown, and the fun of doing a 'Bring me Sunshine' pose by his seafront statue. But few know that he was born in 'the wrong house'! Or that Oliver Cromwell slept in a suit of armour at Stonyhurst College on his way to the decisive battle of Preston. Or that Black Sabbath's rock music pays testimony to Heysham headland's rock-hewn graves. Then there's the story of the two lovers responsible for the knotted larch tree on the promontory called Arnside Knott. And why was the debtors' prison in Lancaster's 'John O' Gaunt's' Castle called 'Hansbrow's Hotel'? There's also the story of Lancaster's slave trade past, the grave of 'Little Sambo', the headless woman in the Priory churchyard, and the unique, self-closing gate in Kirkby Lonsdale.

With all these intriguing tales and many more from locations in and around Lancaster and Morecambe – two places that are like chalk and cheese – this is not your usual guide book. I hope you enjoy exploring its pages and visiting the places covered as much as I enjoyed writing it.

Lindsay Sutton

111 Places

1___ 42 Buxton Street
Eric Morecambe born in 'the wrong house' | 10

2___ 76 Church Street
Did Bonnie Prince Charlie stay here? | 12

3___ Abbey Ruins
Cockersands' monastic marvel on the marsh | 14

4___ Aladdin's Cave of Books
Morecambe's shop without pier | 16

5___ Arnside Pier
Best foot forward for the cross-bay walk to Grange | 18

6___ Arnside Viaduct
So good, they built it thrice! | 20

7___ Ashton Hall
Double death duel with golf club links | 22

8___ Ashton Memorial
Lancaster's Taj Mahal for the love of a woman | 24

9___ Atkinsons Coffee Roasters
Coffee aroma therapy | 26

10___ Bashful Alley
Lancastrians used to swear by the name | 28

11___ Beach Bird 'Indie' Shop
Cornucopia of curios and collectibles | 30

12___ Black and White Canal
Lancaster's 'unkind cut' | 32

13___ Bradford Tram
Next stop, Morecambe Bay coast! | 34

14___ Brucciani's Ice Cream
Sundae Special every day in Morecambe | 36

15___ Butterfly Heaven
Flying high to tie the Knott | 38

16___ Carnforth Station
Brief Encounter film location | 40

17___ Commander Forsberg Sculpture
Marble memorial to Royal Navy hero | 42

18___ Clitheroe Castle
A diabolical liberty with a hole in the wall | 44

19___ Dallam Tower Estate
Milnthorpe's Stately Shelter from the Storm | 46

20___ Debtors' Prison
'Hansbrow's Hotel' pays off | 48

21___ Devil's Bridge
The woman, the cow, the dog and the Devil's pact | 50

22___ Dr Death's House
Scene of the 'jigsaw murders'! | 52

23___ Dunsop Bridge Phone Box
Ringing out for GB Central | 54

24___ Edmondsons Shrimp Shop
Potted history of a Morecambe Bay delicacy | 56

25___ Elizabeth Gaskell Tower
More north than North and South | 58

26___ The Entertainer Theatre
Classical columns lead to a classic film | 60

27___ Eric Gill Mural
Hero and villain of the Midland Hotel | 62

28___ The Failure's Grave
Epitaph leaves more questions than answers | 64

29___ Fairy Steps
Wishful thinking on the corpse trail | 66

30___ Far Arnside Tower
Beware the Border Reivers | 68

31___ *Fireworks and Flags* Mural
Wet and wild at the Midland Hotel | 70

32___ Galgate Silk Mill
Revolution and rhubarb go in the pot | 72

33___ GB Antiques Centre
Cornucopia of collectables and curios | 74

34___ George Fox Bust
Jail Hell Hole for the Quaker maker | 76

35___ George Washington Church
Coat of arms inspires USA's Stars & Stripes | 78

36___ Ghost of the Marsh
Bridal apparition that haunts Bolton-le-Sands | 80

37___ Gillows at Leighton Hall
Please touch the furniture! | 82

38___ Gillow's Mausoleum
Design for the dead | 84

39___ Glasson Dock
The port that saved the Lune | 86

40___ The Golden Lion
A tipple before a topple | 88

41___ Greenway Cycle Route
Pedal power in Morecambe and Lancaster | 90

42___ The Hanging Corner
Stepping through the window of death | 92

43___ Hark to Bounty Inn
Howling dog inspires pub's unusual name | 94

44___ The Headless Lady
Grave concern over woman who beat the clock | 96

45___ Heron Corn Mill
Water power that goes with the grain | 98

46___ Heysham Nature Reserve
Nurturing nature next to the nukes | 100

47___ Heysham Port
Roll up, roll-on, roll-off for Klondike Gold Rush | 102

48___ Inn at Whitewell
Home of the Queen's favourite pub lunch | 104

49___ Jenny Brown's Point
A lady, a lost lover and tales of the sea | 106

50___ The Jigsaw Lounge
Putting the pieces together in Kirkby Lonsdale | 108

51___ John Lawson's Grave
Quaker Meeting House memorial | 110

52___ John O'Gaunt Castle
Where the Queen is toasted as a Duke! | 112

53___ The Judges' Lodgings
Childs' play in Lancaster's hanging house | 114

54___ Kent Estuary Tidal Bore
Surfing USA… that's 'Up Stream Arnside' | 116

55___ Kirkby Lonsdale View
Turner landscape inspires the great 'JR' in 'KL' | 118

56___ Lancaster Brewery
Cheers to local brews made good | 120

57___ Lancaster Grand
Haunting history of theatre's 'Grey Lady' | 122

58___ Lancaster Smokehouse
Haaf way nets success | 124

59___ Levens Hall Topiary
Join the chess set and cut a dash | 126

60___ Little Sambo's Grave
Tragedy of a slave child | 128

61___ Longhouse of Heysham
Lancashire's longhouse tradition lives on | 130

62___ Lovers' Knott Tree
Larch Ascending, high above the Kent Estuary | 132

63___ Lune Estuary Marshes
Nurturing nature, far from the muddying crowd | 134

64___ Lyth Valley
Fruitfulness of the Damson Scene | 136

65___ Market Cross Memorial
Crowning glory of a memorable bus shelter | 138

66___ Marlborough Road
Anthony Newley's route to fame | 140

67___ Morecambe Bay Shrimpers
Nobbies style and whammel wonders | 142

68___ Murals of Morecambe
Gable end art adds a splash of colour | 144

69___ Nuclear Plants
'Energy Central' powers up at the double | 146

70___ Old Poulton
Doorway to the New World | 148

71___ Pennine Tower
Control tower services the M6 | 150

72___ Penny's Almshouses
William Penny for your thoughts | 152

73___ Plover Scar Lighthouse
A flashy and illuminating landmark | 154

74___ The Praying Shell
Sculptor's premonition of cockling tragedy? | 156

75___ Promenade Station
All change for a new Platform | 158

76___ The Radical Steps
Peaceful solution solves pathway problem | 160

77___ Richard Owen Memorial
Terrible lizards, terrible man | 162

78___ Rocking Horse Shop Sign
Things looking up for shop signs of Lancaster | 164

79___ Roman Remains
They didn't 'wery' about the wall | 166

80___ Royal Kings Arms
Dickens of a story with the bride's ghost | 168

81___ The Ruskin
'Love and skill working together – a masterpiece' | 170

82___ Seabird Sculptures
Tern for the better on Morecambe Prom | 172

83___ Settlement of Stydd
A disguised church, almshouses and the Holy Land | 174

84___ Sherlock Holmes' School
An Elementary Connection, my dear Conan Doyle | 176

85___ *SHIP* Sculpture
The art of looking forward and back | 178

86___ Slave Shame Memorial
Captured Africans remembered on Lancaster quay | 180

87___ Snatchems and Catchems
Lune-acy of Lancaster's press gangs | 182

88___ Soul Bowl
Strike it lucky with a ten-pin tonic | 184

89___ Star Café Mural
Mega-market memorial to a lost child | 186

90___ Storey Institute
Stunning spectacle of Lancaster's stained glass | 188

91___ St Mary's Gates
Unique mechanism for – or by – mysterious WG | 190

92___ Stone Igloo
Capturing a 'hole' new horizon | 192

93___ Stonyhurst College
Oliver Cromwell's heavy metal gig at Stonyhurst | 194

94___ The Storey Garden
City-centre orchard bears fruit | 196

95___ St Peter's Viking Grave
Living high on the hogback in Heysham | 198

96___ St Wilfrid's Church
Tolkien's Lord of the Rings *country* | 200

97___ Sunderland Point of Entry
Lancashire's cotton trail began here | 202

98___ Temperance Club
Abstinence makes the tea grow stronger | 204

99___ The Thankful Villages
Great Escape, at the double | 206

100___ Thurnham Hall
Jacobite rebel pays a hefty price | 208

101___ *Time and Tide* Bell
Artwork that dropped a clanger | 210

102___ Trough of Bowland
Pass over Lancashire's Little Switzerland | 212

103___ Trowbarrow Quarry
Ta, Mac, for the limestone | 214

104___ Victoria Wood's Café
One soup… and another soup | 216

105___ The View Café
Morecambe's blasts from the past | 218

106___ V-sign Bridge
I swear that's its name | 220

107___ War Memorial Village
All quiet on the Westfield front | 222

108___ West End Gardens Frame
Picture-perfect seaside scene in Morecambe | 224

109___ The White Bull
'Cheers' to Roman pillars of the community | 226

110___ Winning Post Church
Racehorse victory makes Holy history in Dunsop | 228

111___ Winter Gardens
Where mill girls could be duchesses for the day | 230

1 42 Buxton Street

Eric Morecambe born in 'the wrong house'

It could have come straight from a Morecambe and Wise TV script. As Eric might have said: 'I was born in the wrong house, you know. Right child, wrong house. Oh yes!' Certainly, arrangements for Eric's birth didn't go to plan. A leak in the bedroom roof of the family home at 48 Buxton Street, near Lancaster Road, meant his mother chose to give birth at number 42, home of his aunt. There were no further complications, and Eric Bartholomew came into the world, destined to become one of the country's best-loved comedians, once he had changed his name to Morecambe and teamed up with comedy partner, Ernie Wiseman. Today, celebratory plaques can be found on both of the terraced houses. There's also a third plaque to mark the larger house that the family moved to, in nearby Christie Avenue just a 15-minutes walk away.

Eric's father, George, was an easy-going council labourer, and it was his mother, Sadie, who pushed Eric into developing his entertainment skills. She made sure he could play the piano, and entered young Eric for child talent contests so he would gain experience on stage. Eric met up with Ernie aged just 14, and their comedy double act was born. The partnership would last over 40 years, ending when Eric had a fatal heart attack aged just 58. This was his third attack, and little consolation that his 'grand finale' came after six curtain calls at a charity concert in Tewkesbury, Gloucestershire.

Fittingly, a statue of Eric in classic 'Bring Me Sunshine' dancing pose, was placed on Morecambe's Central Promenade. It was made by Graham Ibbeson, who also produced the Laurel and Hardy statue across the bay in Ulverston. With Eric's catchphrases laid out in front, the statue has become a major attraction on Morecambe's seafront. Such is the warmth of feeling towards this great British comic, that people spend up to 45 minutes posing, singing and dancing beside it.

Address 42 Buxton Street, Morecambe, LA4 5SR | **Getting there** Bus 1A towards
Heysham from Lancaster station; alight at County Garage, then a four-minute walk; by car,
M 6 J 34, then follow the A 683 and B 5321; in Morecambe, take James Street and Charles
Street to Buxton Street | **Hours** Always accessible | **Tip** Eric was a keen birdwatcher –
note the binoculars on his seafront statue – and RSPB Leighton Moss in Silverdale,
North Lancashire, has named a hide and a pool in his memory; Myers Lane, Silverdale,
LA5 0SW – an hour by train from Morecambe to Lancaster, then to Silverdale on the
Barrow train; half an hour by car.

2 _ 76 Church Street

Did Bonnie Prince Charlie stay here?

Lancaster has a rare double link to Bonnie Prince Charlie, one of which is quite illuminating. It's known that the Young Pretender, who aimed to restore the throne to the Stuart dynasty, stayed in Lancaster twice: once when marching south from Scotland with his 7,000-strong army, in November, 1745, and again in December, as they marched back to Scotland, to their ultimate defeat at Culloden. It's widely reported that the Bonnie Prince stayed at 76 Church Street, a fashionable townhouse in the lower part of the city, near to the old bridge over the River Lune. Once rested, the Catholic prince marched south and reached Derby before deciding to head back to Lancaster. From here, he returned to Scotland, where he was routed at Culloden, and fled over the sea to Skye, and on to another period of exile in France.

Number 76 continued to have an interesting existence, being residential, then the headquarter of Lancaster Conservative Association, before being bought by local businessmen. The premises may look classically Georgian in design, but number 76 in fact dates back to Jacobean times, the frontage being but a Georgian façade.

Another interesting detail about number 76 is a rare torch extinguisher 'link', still to be seen outside the splendid porch and doorway of this refurbished Georgian residence. The 'link' is a metal, cone-shaped hood that operates on the same principle as a candle snuffer. At night time, before the advent of 19th-century gas street lighting, a 'link boy' would carry a flaming torch of rags and pitch to light the way for the well-to-do, who were often transported around in Sedan chairs by burly men. In London and Bath, torch links can still be found on buildings, but the Lancaster link is the only one remaining in the city. It's known that Bonnie Prince Charlie went on walkabout in Lancaster, but was it by torchlight or daylight?

Address 76 Church Street, Lancaster, LA1 1ET | Getting there Three-minute walk from
Lancaster bus station or seven-minute walk from Lancaster railway station; by car, from
the south, follow the A6 to the Judges Lodgings | Hours Always visible outside; guided
walks inside available from John Regan (email reganjf@outlook.com) | Tip The Music
Room – a beautiful, hidden Grade II-listed building that was built as a summer pavilion in
number 76's long-vanished garden – now houses a ground-floor coffee shop, but upstairs is a
sumptuous Landmark Trust holiday flat.

3 __ Abbey Ruins

Cockersands' monastic marvel on the marsh

On the often windswept shoreline south of the Lune Estuary is a most unexpected find: the ruins of a 12th-century abbey. This appears to be a most unlikely location for a monastery, until you discover that it grew like Topsy from a simple, one-man hermitage, to an isolation hospital, and finally into the fully-fledged Cockersands Abbey.

Today, almost 900 years after its construction, all that remains of the abbey itself are a few crumbling, low-level walls adjacent to a remote farmhouse. However, beside these ruins is a well-preserved, semi-octagonal Chapter House, which is an intriguing marvel of survival. The abbey was a victim of the Dissolution of the Monasteries in 1539, although a bit of creative accountancy led to an initial three-year stay of execution. Cockersands' books showed it raised just over £157, which was below the initial safety threshold of £200 set by Henry VIII. Revised figures of just above £282 meant it survived, until the 1539 Act swept away all the remaining monasteries – and down went Cockersands. The adjacent Chapter House was saved, as it was used as a burial place for the Dalton family, who lived in nearby Thurnham Hall. This is still open to the public on heritage days, with the listed red sandstone building still an attraction to the public who walk the coastal pathways and past its heavy wooden door.

It's all a far cry from those early days in 1180 when Hugh Garth – said to be 'a hermit of great perfection' – inhabited the lonely spot, inspiring the founding of a hospital for the sick, including lepers. This was enlarged to become a priory, then endowed to become an abbey. Even so, it was still known as St Mary's on the Marshes, before becoming Cockersands Abbey. Whatever the rights and wrongs of the Dissolution, it must have been merciful relief from the cold, harsh environment for the monks who lived there even though it was Lancashire's third richest abbey when dissolved.

Address Near Cockersands Abbey Farm, Lancaster, LA2 0AZ | Getting there Tricky by
car; parking is a problem on the nearby narrow country lanes; the three-mile walk may be
preferable; from Glasson Dock, drive back to the roundabout just outside, turn into School
Lane, which becomes Jeremy Lane, then turn into Moss Lane until you see the farm and
chapel near the coast | Hours Accessible during daylight hours | Tip An evening stroll along
the coast can be sensational for the sun setting over Morecambe Bay, but take care.

4 — Aladdin's Cave of Books
Morecambe's shop without pier

It's estimated that well over 100,000 books are crammed into The Old Pier Bookshop on Morecambe's seafront – but it would be impossible to count them all. As you enter the doorway, there seems to be little order or structure, with unlabelled shelves, crammed alleyways of books, and waist-high piles on the floor. One observer has described the experience as being 'the bibliophile equivalent of cave exploration'. Another comment is that 'the separation of books seems to ebb and flow in an almost hallucinogenic fashion'. However, the books are loosely organised by theme, and the owner, Tony Vettese – known affectionately as 'Mr Bookshop' – is reputedly able to locate request volumes with an uncanny degree of accuracy.

Needless to say, it is an independent bookshop that is family-owned and family-run, and there seems to be a great deal of pride taken in the apparently higgledy-piggledy approach in this warren of second-hand reading material. Printed treasures are to be found, and a couple of hours can flash by as visitors pore over the cornucopia of written material.

Owner Tony is of Scottish-Italian descent, the son of an immigrant from the Abruzzi Mountains in Central Italy, 50 miles inland from Rome. His father set up an ice cream cart business in Glasgow, but in 1961, when Tony was just three years old, the family came to Morecambe, and turned Elsie Binns' lingerie shop into a café. Young Tony eventually brought in his surplus of children's books to sell, with customers then bringing their own. Soon, one corner was given over to them, and eventually the whole shop, and The Old Pier Bookshop was born. More than 30 years later, the business is still going strong, with locals and visitors alike taking great joy in exploring the aisles. Tony has never specialised in any one area or specific topics, and books on all subjects are welcome.

Address 287 Marine Road Central, Morecambe, LA4 5BY, +44 (0)1524 409360 | **Getting there** From the Midland Hotel, a 10-minute walk, east along the seafront Marine Road | **Hours** Daily 10.30am – 6pm | **Tip** Almost opposite the bookshop on the seafront promenade is a rust-coloured steel sculpture depicting and naming the ranges of Cumbrian hills across the bay – perfect to get your bearings.

5 Arnside Pier

Best foot forward for the cross-bay walk to Grange

This unassuming pier projects out into the River Kent, but it's often listed in Britain's Top 20 pier attractions. It's not that long, and has nothing on it, except for park-style furniture and a coin-operated telescope at the T-shaped end. But the views are terrific and therapeutically soothing, especially as the setting sun glints on the water: use the telescope to get close-ups of birdlife, of the far shoreline, and of the Lake District's southern fells and mountains.

The pier actually came about by accident. There was never any intention of building it, until the coast-hugging railway was constructed in 1857, and the long, low viaduct erected across the river. The most suitable point was at the northern end of the small boat-building and fishing village, and though it still looks the picture of elegance, the viaduct meant that the port of Milnthorpe upstream, and the landing point at Sandside, were cut off. In compensation, the railway company built Arnside Pier for unloading goods from the small vessels that plied the coastal waters, and the Irish Sea. The old unloading area timbers can still be seen, beneath the silt on the foreshore, as can the old goods warehouse, now owned by Arnside Yacht Club – a reminder of nautical days both then and now.

The much more solid stone pier of the present day was built to replace the original structure that was destroyed in a fierce gale. But the significance of the pier remains intact: it is the starting point for the guided, cross-bay walks from Arnside to Grange-over-Sands Promenade: three hours one way, three minutes back by train. Charity fund-raising parties, often several hundred strong, are led safely across the potentially-treacherous sands and channels by the Queen's Guide, a historic appointee that dates back to the 16th century, when monks needed safe passage from Furness Abbey to Lancaster.

Address Arnside Promenade, Arnside, Carnforth, LA5 0HA | **Getting there** Half-mile walk from Arnside station, down Station Road and the Promenade; by car, from M6 J35, follow the A6 north, turn left at Milnthorpe traffic lights to Arnside | **Hours** Always accessible; visit www.guideoversands.com for info on cross-bay walks | **Tip** The locally-owned Pier Lane Gallery, on the other side of the road, is an imaginative use of the old library, and has a wonderful collection of local art, photography and craft goods for sale (www.pierlanegallery.com).

6 __ Arnside Viaduct
So good, they built it thrice!

The much-cherished Arnside Viaduct went one better than 'New York, New York', as the famous song has it: Arnside was so good, they built it thrice!

First up was its stunning debut in 1857: it was a thing of beauty; an invaluable transport link for the folk of old north Lancashire and Westmorland – and a nuisance for the small vessels that brought coal and other products to the traditional landing points at Sandsend and Milnthorpe on the upper Kent Estuary. No longer able to navigate past the low 550-foot viaduct with its 50 piers, the railway company paid for a projecting jetty to be built at Arnside – and a new facility and visitor attraction was born.

It was seen as a small price to pay for the benefits of the coast-hugging Cumbrian Coast Line, connecting Barrow-in-Furness with Ulverston, Grange-over-Sands, Arnside, Silverdale and on to the main West Coast Line at Carnforth and Lancaster. The previously isolated communities were at last put on the transport map, with rail links to the whole of England and Scotland. Engineering buffs will also tell you that Arnside Viaduct was the first to use water jets in the construction of the footings. Revolutionary in its day.

Rebuild Number Two came in 1915 at the height of the First World War, when the viaduct needed to be strengthened to carry ammunition trains from Barrow across the Kent, on to the main West Coast Line, and away to the front lines in Europe. The third rebuild was in 2011, when the deck and upper section was replaced, making the passage of trains crossing the estuary much quieter.

For years there's been talk of putting a cycle and walkway on the side of the viaduct, but despite much discussion, for the time being a 14-mile detour to Milnthorpe and around the estuary is needed. Perhaps one day this impressive attraction will benefit from such an addition, shortening the journey to a couple of miles.

Address On the B5282, LA5 OHD | Getting there The obvious way is by train, of course, with the viaduct linking Arnside with Grange-over-Sands; by car, from the M6 J35, head north on the A6 to Milnthorpe, turn left to Arnside | Hours Accessible to see all-year round | Tip Arnside Chip Shop, near the viaduct, is a treat. In good weather, sit and watch the trains cross, and the flowing waters of the River Kent (www.arnsidechipshop.co.uk).

7 __ Ashton Hall

Double death duel with golf club links

Lancaster Golf Club has a relaxed setting in the old parkland surrounding stately Ashton Hall, just a few miles south-west of Lancaster – but it also has a deadly secret. No knife-edge match on the greens could equal the cut and thrust of the notorious duel with swords back in the 18th century, which ended in a double death tragedy.

Early on the morning of 15 November, 1712, the then-owner of Ashton Hall, which is the present-day golfers' clubhouse, mortally wounded his adversary in a do-or-die showdown – only to be fatally wounded himself by his opponent's second. No doubt the scandal was the talk of Lancaster Society, especially since the second then fled the country. Although he was found guilty in his absence, he was later pardoned. Cut and dry, however, was the fact that James, the fourth Lord Hamilton and then owner of Ashton Hall, was dead. The same was true of his adversary, Lord Charles Mohun, who had challenged Hamilton following a disagreement over a property inheritance.

Ultimately, the Hamilton family sold the hall to the wealthy Starkie family from East Lancashire, with major rebuilding taking place before the estate ended up being owned by Lancaster linoleum magnate James Williamson. He took the title Lord Ashton, living in the hall until his death in 1930. His name lives on with the creation of Lancaster's Williamson Park and the Ashton Memorial, and Ashton Hall in Lancaster Town Hall.

Today, Lancaster Golf Club members and visitors can still revel in the notoriety, and enjoy the ambience and marvellous views of the Lune Estuary, the Lake District fells, and the Trough of Bowland. The course itself is one of Lancashire's best, having been laid out in the 1930s by top designer James Braid, a five-times winner of The Open.

Address Lancaster Golf Club, Ashton Hall, Lancaster, LA2 0AJ, +44 (0)1524 751247, www.lancastergc.co.uk, enquiries@lancastergc.co.uk | Getting there 10-minute drive from Lancaster Infirmary off the A6, via Ashton Road; bus 89 to Knott End leaves roughly every 1.5 hours from the infirmary | Hours Daily 7am–6pm | Tip Nearby are the remnants of the old private railway station built solely for Lord Ashton on the long-closed Glasson Dock branch line. It is now the route of the Lancaster Coastal Way for walking and cycling. The station building remains, and the platform can be seen through the track-bed foliage.

8 Ashton Memorial

Lancaster's Taj Mahal for the love of a woman

Lancaster's Ashton Memorial and India's Taj Mahal may be architectural opposites, but they were both built for the love of a woman. The baroque-style Ashton Memorial was constructed on top of a commanding hill above Lancaster as a tribute to local industrialist, Lord Ashton's late wife, Jesse; the Taj Mahal was built by Moghul Emperor Shah Jahan as a token of love for his beloved Mumtaz, in a style that reflected Indian, Persian and Mogul architecture. Both buildings still impress, and both are focal points in their respective cities of Lancaster and Aggra. In Lancaster, the 54-acre Williamson Park that surrounds the Ashton Memorial is used by Lancastrians as a playground, to take in the commanding views from the memorial's 360-degree viewing arena, to visit the Butterfly House and the Mini Zoo, or to relax over tea and buns in the Pavilion Café.

The Grade I-listed building, finished in 1909, is built from the finest Portland Stone, with Cornish granite steps, and a huge copper dome that can be seen from afar, even from the passing M 6. It is 150 feet high, and offers magnificent views of the city, the surrounding countryside, and of Morecambe Bay and the Lakeland fells and mountains.

It's pleasing to know that the man behind the memorial, industrialist James Williamson II, was a shy and private individual, who was not without his human frailties. He grew his father's textile-related business to become a leading producer of linoleum, leather cloth and coated fabrics, employing a quarter of all working men in Lancaster. He was known as the 'Lion King of Lancaster', and became the city's Liberal MP, on a platform of free trade and Home Rule for Ireland. He had a strong philanthropic nature, but was obsessed with time-keeping. The local joke was that he built the memorial as a vantage point to see that his workers arrived on time at his factory down below.

Address Quernmore Road, Lancaster, LA1 1UX, +44 (0)1524 33318, williamsonpark@lancaster.gov.uk | Getting there From the Lune Bridge, travel south on the A6, taking a left up Moor Lane, which becomes Wyresdale Road; parking available at top of hill for £2 a day; bus 18 from Lancaster station | Hours Park open summer 10am–5pm, winter 10am–4pm | Tip Golgotha, the evocative Biblical name of an area on the edge of Williamson Park, was the spot where Lancaster's many hangings took place prior to 1800. Today, the old stone stocks that were clamped on miscreants' legs remain in situ.

9 Atkinsons Coffee Roasters
Coffee aroma therapy

The long-running 'Battle of the Beverages' between tea and coffee rages on, but whatever the long-term outcome in the popularity stakes, there's one producer in Lancaster that's sure to come out tops. J. Atkinson & Co has been supplying both commodities since Queen Victoria's accession to the throne in 1837. Not only does Atkinsons straddle the great tea and coffee divide, the company also incorporates old and new in terms of production technology and use of digital technology. Its teas go back to the days of the East India Company, while the coffees embrace the latest barista culture.

The shop itself, located in the city centre on China Street, is a real blast from the past, from its traditional pavement frontage to the characterful interior, with a mahogany counter made by renowned Lancaster furniture designer Gillows, along with rows of huge jars and metal containers on the shelves behind. Near the window, the old grinding machine continues to operate, dispersing the aroma of fresh coffee through the extractor fan to entice passers-by outside. At the rear of the shop, however, you can see the latest state-of-the-art machinery. What you might call, a perfect blend of old and new!

The firm's founder, Thomas Atkinson saw the need for quality beverages, and was in an ideal position to grow the market on both fronts. Today, he would no doubt be pleased to know that customers can savour the vintage atmosphere of the shop, while taking tea or coffee next door in The Hall – formerly the locality's Parish Hall. It's impossible to know whether Thomas would be surprised that our 'nation of tea drinkers' now consume 95 million cups of coffee a day, compared to 165 million cups of tea. Old Tom's continued growth in popularity is unsurprising given the cultural influences of both America and continental Europe, and the explosion of coffee shops with WIFI.

Address 12 China Street, Lancaster, LA1 1EX, +44 (0)1524 65470, www.thecoffeehopper.com | Getting there Train to Lancaster station; by car, from M6 J33, follow signs for Lancaster on the A6 north, becoming China Street in the city | Hours Mon–Sat 9am–5pm, Sun 9am–4pm | Tip Atkinsons runs another café on the ground floor of the nearby Grade I-listed Music Room, a one-time 18th-century summer house with a Palladian façade, located in nearby Sun Street.

10_Bashful Alley

Lancastrians used to swear by the name

Bashful Alley is a cut-through and a name that certainly intrigues – especially if you know what it used to be called. As an original haunt of sailors and prostitutes back in the boom-town Lancaster of the 18th century, it had a specific purpose that isn't hard to guess. As males and females changed partners, it earned the rather unsavoury nickname of 'Swap Fanny Alley' (or words to that effect…).

Unsurprisingly, someone came up with the more refined name for the ginnel that connects the top of Market Street to the bottom end of King Street. The more sanitised explanation of the present-day tag is that in the 19th century, bashful young women could use the cut-through to avoid the unwanted attention of rowdy young men, who would congregate outside the pubs at the crossroads that linked Market Street with King Street and China Street, both on the main A6 route through the town. So it is that Bashful Alley is talked of locally as the street with two different names, spanning two different centuries, and having two different stories.

Since those Georgian and Victorian days, Bashful Alley has changed dramatically, being now safe and secure, and with a decided switch to health and welfare. Today, the alley houses a centre devoted to pain and stress relief that deals with helping people regain control of their physical, intellectual and emotional well-being. The Alexander Technique centre is based on an approach developed by Australian Frederick Matthias Alexander, who worked to overcome personal problems brought on by the stress and strain of his life. He came to London in the early 20th century, and his coping techniques live on in the heart of Lancaster. However, if a cup of tea is your way of coping, The Old Bell Café is a classic 'hidden gem,' serving all-day breakfasts and lovely cakes. Just round the corner, the coach and horses bound for Manchester left the old Sir Simon's Inn – a seven-hour journey back in the early 19th century.

Address King Street, Lancaster, LA1 1LF | **Getting there** From Lancaster Castle Gatehouse, it's a four-minute walk down Lancaster Hill and into Market Street | **Tip** Another town centre alley is Ffrances Passage, a double 'f' signifying a capital 'F' before there was a common written form. Named after 'John ffrance,' the family sold the passageway to the corporation, and it has become a well-used public thoroughfare.

11 Beach Bird 'Indie' Shop

Cornucopia of curios and collectibles

There's magic in the air when you walk into Morecambe's seafront Beach Bird shop. And that's before you even get to the dedicated magician's section at the back of the premises. From opening the front door, the whole place is full of an eclectic range of 'curiosities and collectibles', as the shop's mantra has it.

The 'indie', run by a local husband and wife partnership, Moira and Andy Winters, together with friend Jane Wignall, was set up to support local artists, authors, makers and artisans, providing an outlet for their work. Things took off from there, and now the range of goods and creative work has grown considerably, as the owners follow the approach of 19th-century arts and crafts designer, William Morris, who advised: 'Have nothing in your houses that you do not know to be useful or believe to be beautiful.'

The shop is a cornucopia of delight, offering jewellery to journals; handbags to tote bags; cushions to candles; and a wide range of ear rings made from wire, mosaics, and even feathers. Re-purposed items can include funky lamps, clocks set in car hubcaps, and even a talking ape head. The owners are adamant that this is 'more than just a shop', because they 'value individuality and a sense of fun and creativity'. Their proud claim is that they 'support local, because we are local'.

The shop front itself is pleasing to the eye. The beautiful, curved glass and wood frontage is shared with the Temperance Club Barbers, which still has the old name above the door. On the real magic front, at the rear of Beach Bird, is the actual magic section, which has a range of displays and items for sale. This area is the preserve of Andy, whose offerings include Madam Zelda's scratch-card predictions, which highlight life, love and fortune, and the work of Carter the Great, the World's Weird and Wonderful Wizard, plus a Store Alarm Prank, which sounds rather anti-social.

Address Beach Bird, 240a Marine Road Central, Morecambe, LA4 4BJ, www.beachbird.co.uk |
Getting there Short walk along Marine Road Central from the Midland Hotel | Hours
Tue–Sun 11am–4pm | Tip Five minutes' walk away is a fascinating arts and crafts supplies
shop called 'Little Shop of Hobbies', run by a mother and daughter team in Pedder Street,
just off the seafront.

12 Black and White Canal

Lancaster's 'unkind cut'

In its heyday, the Lancaster Canal earned the nickname 'The Black and White Canal'. It took coal north and limestone south, and helped put both Lancaster and Kendal on the map. Inevitably, the coming of the railway in the 19th century, and the massively-improved road network of the 20th century, killed off its industrial necessity.

However, instead of having the foresight to see the 'Northern Reaches' as a leisure and tourist attraction, it was allowed to fall into disrepair. Worse still, the canal was cut in three places by the construction of the M6 in the 1970s, and by the A590 near Kendal – a source of regret ever since. Rather like the Beeching cuts to the railways, there was little vision, and Kendal was left with a 14-mile section of waterway going nowhere. It remains a partial route for walkers and cyclists, and the southern section is still used by pleasure boats. Being a contour canal, and following the lay of the land instead of using locks and massive embankments, the views from many sections are magnificent – and there are major attempts to link up again with the northern section.

When the 'Lancaster' was built back in the late 18th century, the 57-mile-long 'cut' stretched from Preston to Kendal, with only one set of locks at Tewitfield near Carnforth, this being the current end of today's navigable waterway. It was first used in 1797, and completed in 1826, with a spur being constructed to Glasson Docks, down river from Lancaster, affording lock entry to the River Lune and the Irish Sea. As such, it was a gateway between the Old World and the New World, taking manufactured goods from Lancashire and Yorkshire to America. Before the railway, 'packet boats' offered an 'express' canal passenger service between Lancaster and Preston, and later on up to Kendal. It took almost eight hours, but that halved the fastest speed of the stagecoach. Then came the advent of the train, and canals were on the way out.

Address Aldcliffe Road Mooring in Lancashire, LA1 1AZ, is a central point | Getting there 15-minute walk from Lancaster station | Hours Accessible all year round | Tip Take a two-hour, return Kingfisher barge cruise from the Aldcliffe Road Mooring in Lancaster to the Lune Aqueduct, the impressive 18th-century structure that carries the canal over the river (May to October, www.kingfishcruise.co.uk).

13 Bradford Tram

Next stop, Morecambe Bay coast!

It's not something you expect to see… the remains of an old Bradford tram, decomposing in its seaside setting at the edge of a salt marsh. It's now just a pile of rotting wood, but it's the symbolic story behind it that is fascinating to walkers between Sunderland Point and Heysham.

The 120-year-old tramcar was one of several brought over from West Yorkshire half a century ago to use as cheap holiday homes on the Morecambe Bay coast. Today, only one tram survives, and its wrecked remains stand as a memory of the 'Wakes Week' holidays of working families from the industrial mill towns. With a direct railway line from West Yorkshire through Skipton and Lancaster, it is little wonder that Morecambe itself was called 'Little Bradford'. It remains a retirement favourite for many Bradford folk.

The remaining Bradford tram, said to be Number 223, was on the tracks from 1901 until 1950, when the tramlines were ripped up, to be replaced by an expanded trolley bus system in the old West Riding's worsted wool citadel. A few of the redundant trams were initially on a holiday site nearer to Heysham until they were replaced once more, this time by caravans. A local farmer bought one of the trams and moved it to a field nearer to the Lune Estuary. Its life as a holiday home ended as the tram deteriorated: all that remains is the hardwood frame of the old tramcar.

The location of the old, decomposing tram is what most seaside landladies call 'bracing', which is a euphemism for 'windy'. Certainly, the walking route up the coast is open to the prevailing west winds, and that's after you have braved the tidal passage to Sunderland Point, north of the River Lune. After trekking past Sambo's Grave, you feel open to the seascape of Morecambe Bay and on through the fields to the site near Hargreaves Farm. It's healthy, but some say, the end of the line.

Address Near Hargreaves Farm, LA3 3HP | Getting there By car, from Heysham: follow Middleton Road towards Overton, right into Carr Road to Shore-fields Caravan Site, then down the coastal lane to Hargreaves Farm | Hours Daylight all year round | Tip Walking north along the coast towards Heysham is a gated community of bungalows and apartments. Amazing to think this was once the huge Pontins' Holiday Camp, complete with theatre and entertainment centre, shaped like an ocean liner.

14 Brucciani's Ice Cream

Sundae Special every day in Morecambe

It's a much-loved part of Morecambe's identity, loved and cherished by locals and visitors alike. But Brucciani's ice cream parlour only ended up in the resort by accident, and by chance. The business, still going strong in its nationally-listed Art Deco premises on the seafront, was set up initially in the town by a Glasgow-based Italian family who were thinking of setting up down the coast in Blackpool. However, as patriarch Peter Leo Brucciani headed south from Scotland, he took a wrong turn… and ended up in Morecambe!

He liked what he saw in the booming holiday centre of the late 19th century, and so he opened up an ice cream shop in the town's West End, back in 1893. Forty six years on, his son Bruno opened the present Brucciani's on the seafront on Marine Road West. It still stands there, popular as ever, exactly as it was when the doors opened on September 2nd, 1939, the day before World War II broke out. It may not have been the best opening date, especially for an Italian family, but Bruno kept open during the war, and Brucciani's has been an institution that survives to this day.

The family-run business is a temple of Poirot-style taste, an architectural and culinary experience to savour, every bit as much as the 1930s Midland Hotel (see ch. 27) just along the promenade. Top-class coffee, cream and ices are still its major offerings, with Knickerbocker Glories, Banana Splits and Sundaes still all-time favourites. The simple, clean lines of the parlour's interior are still a joy to locals and visitors alike. Brown wood, chrome, black lacquer panels, porthole windows, Ziggurat-style doors and classic door handles all help set the authentic 1930s feel – and it's the real thing. Sadly, Bruno died in 2020, just short of his 90th birthday, but his children Cristina, Peter and Paulo keep up the tradition. The original ethos has been preserved.

Address 217 Marine Road West, Morecambe, LA4 4AX, +44 (0)1524 412000, info@bruccianiicecream.com | **Getting there** Four-minute walk from Morecambe's seafront Midland Hotel | **Hours** Sat & Sun 10am–4pm, check Facebook page for more details | **Tip** A five-minute walk away, on Euston Road, is Wetherspoon's The Eric Bartholomew pub that serves beer and cheer, just like the comedian who changed his surname to that of his home town of Morecambe (www.jdwetherspoon.com).

15 Butterfly Heaven
Flying high to tie the Knott

Arnside Knott – the imposing hill overlooking the Kent Estuary above Arnside itself (see ch. 5) – is renowned for its magnificent seascape views. Stretching out below are the ever-changing vistas across Morecambe Bay, with the Lakeland mountains and fells in the far distance.

However, it's the walk on the wild side of the Knott that is equally impressive. It's a butterfly Heaven on earth, and is said to support the most species in the whole of northern England. Experts point out the unique circumstances that attract and encourage 34 different species to frequent the area, with all but three of these being residents. Lepidopterists, the name for those with butterfly expertise, highlight the coming together of the coastal climate; the limestone pavement terrain, with its exposed slabs and deep, protective cracks between them, and the grassland and varied woodland of the area. These may be relatively constant, but in today's dynamic and ever-changing climate and weather conditions, butterfly numbers can vary considerably. Annual figures can be up and down tenfold, but the butterfly seems to keep bouncing back.

The names of some of the 34 recorded species range from the amusing to the intriguing: from the Dingy Skipper to the Duke of Burgundy, from the High-Brown Fritillary to the Northern Brown Angus, from the White-Letter Hairstreak to the Painted Lady. All are to be found on Arnside Knott, in neighbouring Myers Allotments in Silverdale, and also on Warton Crags near Carnforth to the south.

Warm, sunny days are best for sightings, but the various species can be seen resting on dull days. However, there is no complacency. The Arnside Area of Outstanding Natural Beauty and the Butterfly Conservation movement are working hard on habitat management in the locality, seeking to enhance and extend the special conditions on which the butterflies depend.

Address Arnside Knott car park, Carnforth, LA5 0BP | **Getting there** By car, from Silverdale Road, Arnside, turn right into Red Hills Road. Half a mile on, keep left on to Knott Lane, then Saul's Drive; take the track, cross the cattle grid to the car park | **Hours** Daytime all-year round | **Tip** The two-hour, circular walk up and around Arnside Knott is spectacular and fascinating. The 'moderate' walk is 1.7 miles, taking in 400-year-old woodlands, and offering awesome views over Morecambe Bay.

16 Carnforth Station

Brief Encounter *film location*

Brief Encounter remains one of Britain's best-loved films, even though it's more than 75 years since it was first released. The classic love story took place in a railway station – a 'brief encounter' that threatened to break up two marriages. The real-life railway station where it was filmed is at Carnforth, just ten miles north of Lancaster. It not only put the old industrial town on the map, but also made it a permanent visitor attraction in itself.

The station refreshment room, where love blossomed following the chance meeting of Doctor Alec Harvey, played by Trevor Howard, and housewife Laura Jesson, played by Celia Johnson, remains a café. Other platform premises have been turned into Carnforth Station Heritage Centre, attracting thousands of visitors a year. You can savour the atmosphere of 1945, when the film was shot by David Lean, the celebrated director who masterminded the other classics, *Lawrence of Arabia* and *Doctor Zhivago*.

Trains still flash by on the main London to Scotland West Coast Line; but stop on the Lancaster to Barrow line round Morecambe Bay, and on the Skipton to Lancaster route that brought thousands of Yorkshire mill workers on holiday to Morecambe. The Victorian-era station, Milford Junction in the film, is authentic enough. On Platform 1, outside the old waiting room, is an old handcart, complete with vintage brown leather suitcases, and classic, old-style railway posters on the wall.

Once inside the Heritage Centre, there is an abundance of railway memorabilia that's of interest not only to railway enthusiasts, but for nostalgia and film buffs too. You can even watch the actual film, which runs 1,500 times a year, while sitting on plush, tip-up seats in the vintage mini cinema. You might even wipe a speck of dust from a lady's eye! It's all run by volunteers, and although admission is free, donations are appreciated.

Address Warton Road, Carnforth, LA5 9TR | **Getting there** Train to Carnforth station; by car, M6 J35, then follow Carnforth signs on the A6 | **Hours** Mon–Fri 10am–4pm | **Tip** Carnforth Book Shop is an independent, family-run jewel in the heart of Carnforth that has operated for approaching 50 years; it's just a few minutes' walk from the station at the top of Market Street; downstairs are new books and gifts, while upstairs has second-hand and antiquarian books and maps (www.carnforthbooks.co.uk).

17 Commander Forsberg Sculpture

Marble memorial to Royal Navy hero

You might expect a Morecambe resident not to be 'all at sea' when it comes to swimming: Commander Gerry Forsberg was certainly in control. The captain of no less than five destroyers during his 40 years in the Royal Navy, Forsberg was organised, thorough in his planning, and resolute in action. He swam almost every day in Morecambe Bay, off the West End Gardens, whenever he was back in his adopted town. He swam across to Kent's Bank in present-day Cumbria no less than 29 times during his 88 years, and in 1959 completed the two-way swim of 18 miles in an inaugural record time of six hours 23 minutes.

The marble figure of him in action is there for all to see, on the very spot where he would get into the water, just opposite his marital home in Ervine Terrace. The sculpting shows him immersed in the sea, only his head (wearing goggles) and one arm, above water. It's fitting testimony to a man who clocked up well over 13,000 miles, swimming the oceans, lakes and lochs in and around Britain. And so it went on – Commander Forsberg broke records in 1958 and 1959 in Windermere (21 miles), Northern Ireland's Loch Neagh, taking the diagonal he felt to be the longest (19.4 miles), Loch Lomond (21.6 miles), and in 1959, the Morecambe Bay two-way record. Before all this, in 1957, at the age of 45, Forsberg broke the cross-Channel swim record, beating the previous best time by 22 minutes. Following these achievements he became President of the British Long Distance Swimming Association in 1963.

Following his long and distinguished Royal Navy career, Forsberg became a salvage expert, bringing up a De Havilland Comet from the seabed, thereby helping experts to solve the cause of a structural weakness that was causing deadly crashes. He was awarded the OBE, among his many other accolades, before his death in 2000.

Address Opposite Regent Road on Morecambe Promenade, Morecambe, LA3 1BU | Getting there 10-minute walk from the Midland Hotel | Hours Always accessible | Tip See the array of artworks designed by local artists in the West End Gardens, including the 10-metre-high Fishing Rod and Hook, the collection of horns and the giant picture frame.

18 Clitheroe Castle

A diabolical liberty with a hole in the wall

The 12th-century castle, built on a limestone outcrop, is still a majestic sight in the heart of the town. It has stunning views of the surrounding Ribble Valley and was bought by public subscription in 1920 as a memorial to locals killed in the First World War. But like the bridge near Kirkby Lonsdale (see ch. 55), legend has it that the hole in the castle's wall was the work of the Devil!

According to this tale, the Devil gathered an apron full of rocks on the side of nearby Pendle Hill, and attempted to hurl them towards the town of Clitheroe. But the apron broke, most of the rocks fell out, and only one was hurled, hitting the castle wall. It's an exciting story, but the truth is more prosaic. It's reported that on Thomas Cromwell's orders, his Roundhead-controlled local militia breached the castle wall during the English Civil War, in order to stop Clitheroe ever becoming a Royalist stronghold. Yet another fanciful tale has it that Cromwell himself stood on Pendle Hill and ordered his cannon to fire at the castle. This begs the question, why would he go up the steep hill in the first place, when his only quest during the one time he passed through, was to engage with the Royalists and Scots near Preston? Besides, a Civil War-era cannon could fire its cannonball less than a mile – far less than the two miles or so distance from the hill.

Another version of the Devil story says the boulder thrown fell short, landing near the church in the village of Pendleton: there's still a pile of rocks on Pendle Hill that is called the 'Apronfull', which you can see if you travel over the Nick o' Pendle – the twisting pass between Clitheroe and Sabden village. The rocks are just a short walk uphill, after crossing the road from Pendle Dry Ski Slope. They may seem unlikely tales, but who wants to be a myth-buster, extinguishing the spark of these dramatic stories? An interesting mix of fact, fiction and folklore bound up in one castle.

Address Castle Hill, Clitheroe, BB7 1BA, +44 (0)1200 424568, clitheroecastle@lancashire.gov.uk | Getting there By car, from M 6 J 31, follow the Blackburn, then Clitheroe signs on the A 59; from Lancaster station, one hour by car; 10-minute walk from Clitheroe bus and railway stations | Hours Castle and grounds open daily 9am–5pm, museum Fri–Tue noon–4pm | Tip A two-hour, five-mile circular walk takes in Clitheroe town and Pendleton village, with views of Pendle Hill and the Ribble Valley (www.visitlancashire.com).

19 Dallam Tower Estate

Milnthorpe's Stately Shelter from the Storm

The sight of a huge herd of deer grazing peacefully by the gently-flowing River Bela is impressive – and so is the classically-designed deer shelter. It's not every day you see a deer herd given such five-star treatment, their shelter featuring Tuscan columns to support the surrounding canopy. Not surprisingly, the pillared, Georgian building is Grade II listed.

Dallam Tower is a private country home built in the 18th century, with additions and remodelling over the following two centuries. The deer park of 190 acres also contains a 'reservoir' built to attract ducks for shoot outings. In the early 1720s, the estate was acquired by the obviously-wealthy Wilson family, with both Daniel Wilson and his son Edward representing the old county of Westmorland as Members of Parliament. The house has membership of the Historic Houses Association, but isn't open to the public, except for occasional charity events and visits to the garden under the National Gardens Scheme. In the 14th century, a defensive Pele tower was sited on what is now the deer park, near to the river, but this was demolished when the present house was built between 1720 and 1723. At least two ocean-going vessels were named the Dallam Tower, both of which came to grief. The first, built in nearby Milnthorpe, ran aground and broke up en route from Dublin to Whitehaven, up the Cumbrian coast. The second, which was registered in Lancaster, was wrecked off Java, while carrying coal from Newcastle to the Far East.

The herd of deer and their stately shelter can often be seen from the A6, between Milnthorpe and Beetham village, the riverside lay-by providing a perfect vantage point to take in the beautiful view across the River Bela. The deer roam free alongside sheep on the Dallam Tower Estate, which has a public footpath running through it, so walkers can enjoy the peaceful, riverside scene.

Address Dallam Tower Estate, Milnthorpe, near Carnforth, LA7 7AG | **Getting there** A6 lay-by on the left, half a mile outside Beetham going north | **Hours** Always accessible | **Tip** St Anthony's Tower is a grey-stone edifice on a hilltop east of the A6, just north of Milnthorpe; built by a Henry Smithies to commemorate the 1832 Reform Act, it is a commanding spectacle, but located on private land with no public access.

20 Debtors' Prison

'Hansbrow's Hotel' pays off

Lancaster Castle may have had a fearsome reputation for hangings (see ch. 42), but for debtors it was called 'Hansbrow's Hotel'. Not exactly five-star, but light years from the felons' dungeons down below. A far cry, too, from the harsh realities of Marshalsea Debtors' Prison on the south bank of the Thames in London, well chronicled by Charles Dickens in *Little Dorrit*.

Debtors in Lancaster were required to work within the prison, in return for provisions, with any surplus being used to help pay off their debts. At any one time there would be between 300 and 400 people 'incarcerated', though the freedoms they were afforded were humane and generous. This was courtesy of Captain James Hansbrow, Prison Governor between 1833 and 1862 – a period not exactly known for an enlightened or sensible approach.

Debtors at 'Hansbrow's' worked in the Clockhouse, which was on the ground level, with views out on to the castle courtyard. If they had access to money – and were maybe waiting for a property sale to pay off their debts – life could be better still. They had a choice of 22 rooms, priced between five and 30 shillings (25p and £1.50). The fee included the provision of a fire, candles, cooking utensil, and even the service of a 'room man', who would cook and clean.

Debtors could buy beer, wine and tobacco, though no spirits. They could purchase food, clothing and newspapers, continue to follow their trade or profession, and have visitors between 8am and 8pm. They could also play games in the courtyard, where imprisoned musicians often organised soirées and dances. A Debtors' Market was held, and meat and poultry, fish, vegetables and fruit could be purchased. There are tales of concerts, fairs, social clubs, and even mock elections bring held. Providing there was an ultimate way to pay off one's debts, it was probably better than being free on the outside!

Address Lancaster Castle, Castle Parade, LA1 1YN | Getting there Five-minute walk from Lancaster station; by car, parking is available in Dallas Road Car Park | Hours Courtyard access is free 9.30am–5pm | Tip Lancaster Cottage Museum, just down Castle Hill from Lancaster Castle, transports you to 18th-century life in a humble dwelling in the heart of the old city (www.visitlancaster.org.uk/museum).

21 Devil's Bridge

The woman, the cow, the dog and the Devil's pact

The name Devil's Bridge certainly intrigues, and begs the question: why is it called that? As you might expect, the explanation, according to folklore in and around Kirkby Lonsdale (see ch. 55), is fascinating. The three-arched, stone structure is beautifully proportioned and sturdily built to withstand the fierce torrent of the River Lune, 17 miles upstream from Lancaster. But the story behind it is a tale of a pact with the Devil, that ended with the triumph of 'right' over 'might'.

The bridge is said to date back to the 12th century, when there was no safe way across the Lune. According to legend, an old woman who lived on one of the banks woke up one morning to find that one of her cows had managed to get to the other side, but could not be coaxed or cajoled into making the perilous return journey.

The Devil appeared to her and offered a deal: he would build her a bridge in return for the soul of the first body to cross the structure. The woman agreed, and the Devil built it with his own hands, leaving his handprint on the stone at the apex – a 'sign' that can be seen to this day. The woman met the Devil and agreed to fulfil her part of the bargain, but she had a small dog with her, and when she threw a bun across the bridge, the dog ran across, thereby forfeiting its soul. The Devil was outraged at not obtaining the soul of a human. According to the tale, he howled in fury, then disappeared in a cloud of brimstone, leaving the bridge to be used by locals and travellers alike.

Today, the narrow bridge is no longer used by vehicles, having been replaced by the modern A 65 bridge, carrying traffic from Yorkshire to the Lakes. Ten miles away, near High Bentham, on the edge of the Trough of Bowland, is a huge boulder called The Great Stone of Fourstones. One folklore tale has it that this was dropped by the Devil on his way to build Devil's Bridge.

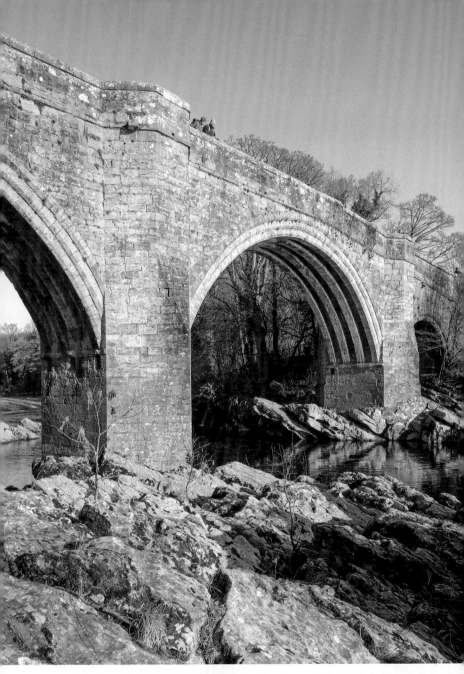

Address Kirby Lonsdale, LA6 2DF | **Getting there** 15-minute walk from Market Square; parking is available at Bridge Brow | **Hours** Always accessible | **Tip** Enjoy an artisanal Italian ice cream at The Milking Parlour, a family-run farm business whose slogan is 'Cow to Cone'; the ice cream is made daily and sold from their premises (www.cowtocone.co.uk).

22 Dr Death's House
Scene of the 'jigsaw murders'!

Lancaster's fine architecture is reflected in the façade of 2 Dalton Square – but within this building, the haunting memories of a one-time 'House of Horror' live on. It was here that, in 1935, highly-respected surgeon, Dr Buck Ruxton, perpetrated what came to be known as the 'Jigsaw Murders'. Ruxton slaughtered his common-law wife Isabella, and the couple's live-in housemaid Mary Jane Rogerson – then dismembered them both. Using the family bath, Ruxton clinically cut them up into 70 pieces, wrapping them in clothing and newspaper, before putting the pieces in four large bags. He then drove north and threw the bags into a stream near Moffat in the Scottish hills.

A fortnight later, a female hiker was crossing a bridge when she spotted a human arm down below. She alerted the police, and a landmark investigation began. The body parts – including two heads – were painstakingly put together, and the age of maggots in the body parts proved that they were dumped less than two weeks earlier.

The case proved to be the birth of modern forensics. However, a major factor in bringing Ruxton to justice was finding that a newspaper page he'd used was from Lancaster's *Sunday Graphic*, dated 15 September, 1935. Checking missing persons, Lancaster police noted that Ruxton had reported that his wife and maid had disappeared. The maid's parents verified that a blouse found with the body parts belonged to their daughter; when a photo of Isabella was superimposed on to one of the skulls, it matched perfectly.

Upon his arrest, Ruxton denied the murders, but accepted that he was consumed with jealousy over his wife's alleged affairs with members of Lancaster's 'town hall set'. He was tried, found guilty, and hanged at Manchester's Strangeways Prison. For decades, his home remained unsellable, until the council's planning department gutted it, and moved in.

Address 2 Dalton Square, Lancaster, LA1 1PN | Getting there Six-minute walk from Lancaster bus station | Hours Always visible externally | Tip To escape the rigours of the Ruxton murders, try a lunchtime organ recital at Lancaster Town Hall's Ashton Hall, nearby in Dalton Square, which has a rare Norman and Beard Organ from Norwich (www.ahorp.org).

23 __ Dunsop Bridge Phone Box
Ringing out for GB Central

The day when BT put a telephone box in little Dunsop Bridge was a red-letter day for the village post office. BT put up a plaque in the box near the post office-cum-café, announcing that the spot was the geographical centre of Britain. The Ordnance Survey, Britain's national mapping agency, verified it, and the adventurer Sir Ralph Fiennes was engaged to open the public telephone box officially. And to mark the opening of BT's 100,000th phone box, a depiction of the four points of the compass was put on the floor. At the post office, trade increased, as intrigued visitors came to the village, which is just 15 miles from the heart of Lancaster, travelling across the scenic and spectacular Trough of Bowland pass. The little hamlet on the Hodder was well and truly on the map.

That was back in 1992, but after that things began to unravel. For starters, satellite mapping techniques showed the actual dead centre was 4.5 miles away, on Brennand Farm, near the ominously-named Whitendale Hanging Rocks. And pretty soon, three counter claims were made – one from the town of Haltwhistle, near Hadrian's Wall in Northumberland; another from Meriden, near Coventry; and finally, a claim that the spot was in a field on Lindley Hall Farm in Ferry Drayton, Leicestershire.

There's little harm done with the rivalry, even though Dunsop Bridge rather likes the reflected glory. In any case, the Queen likes to pop in when she's staying in the area in her official capacity as Duke of Lancaster. She has enjoyed a cup of tea in Puddleducks Café, which is inside the post office, and she no doubt feeds the ducks which congregate on the banks of the River Hodder outside. She often stays locally, and genuinely loves the area. Perhaps she'll be back at Puddleducks soon, to enjoy the thick pea and ham soup… even the Lancashire Hotpot. No such comfort for the Pendle Witches who passed this way for their Lancaster trial in 1612.

Address Dunsop Bridge Post Office, Clitheroe, BB7 3BB | **Getting there** Half-hour drive from Lancaster city centre; follow Wyresdale Road, which becomes Langthwaite Road, on through Quernmore and on to Dunsop Bridge | **Hours** Daytime hours at Puddleducks Café / post office | **Tip** The seven-mile circular walk from Dunsop Bridge to the village of Newton and back is a strollers' favourite, with public toilets and Puddleducks Café at the start, and the Parkers Arms in Newton at the half-way mark.

24 Edmondsons Shrimp Shop
Potted history of a Morecambe Bay delicacy

Potted shrimps and Morecambe Bay. They go together, like cattle and hay. Like the horse and carriage. Like love and marriage. Like nuts and raisins. Like Fortnum and Masons. Forgive my poetic licence, but the point is made: Bay shrimps really are something special in these parts. Cooked in hot butter, then sealed and potted in solidified butter, they can still be savoured in Morecambe. However, whereas shrimps were once an abundant harvest, they are now drastically down in numbers. Once, there were 30-odd Morecambe shrimp boats, but now only a couple remain.

Ray Edmondson, now in his 70s, is one of the last shrimp fishermen, and his family runs Edmondson's Fresh Fish Shop in Yorkshire Street, in Morecambe's West End. It's a traditional wet fish shop that gives locals and visitors alike the chance to connect with the sea's bounty first hand. Apart from shrimp, the array of produce is impressive: it includes Manx kippers, Aberdeen haddock, as well as cod, hake, halibut, sea bass, trout and salmon, though low stocks mean Lune salmon is currently outlawed.

It's the shrimp that's symbolically the essence of Morecambe Bay, however, and though Ray's vessel is showing its age, the *Bernadette* still does the job. Its traditional trawl net skims along the shallows, scooping up shrimp, and sometimes the occasional plaice and flounder as well. Once aboard, the shrimps are boiled in sea water before being taken ashore. At the shop, they are boiled in butter, along with a secret combination of spices. By now, the once-brown shrimps have turned pink, and once they've cooled, they're potted with the butter which solidifies around them. This Morecambe delicacy can be served warm or cold, eaten as a starter or a light meal with salad, or even on toast or crusty bread. Hotels often include shrimp in afternoon tea offerings, and there's still demand for them in local tea rooms.

Address 32A Yorkshire Street, West End, Morecambe, LA3 1QE, +44 (0)1524 412828, www.edmondsonspottedshrimps.co.uk | Getting there 15-minute walk from Morecambe railway station | Hours Mon & Tue, Thu–Sat 9am–4pm, Wed 9am–12.30pm | Tip For cooked fish and chips, try Atkinson's in nearby Albert Road: locals and visitors alike have enjoyed their fare for well over a century (www.atkinsonsfishandchips.co.uk).

25 Elizabeth Gaskell Tower

More north than North and South

Silverdale's rather striking and unusual Lindeth Tower was built as a rich man's summer house, but quickly served as a writing retreat for Elizabeth Gaskell. The Manchester-based author of Mary Barton, Cranford and North and South, wrote her novel *Ruth* and some of her work for *The Life of Charlotte Brontë* over summer months spent at Lindeth, soon after it was built in 1842. Mrs Gaskell would go on to become highly acclaimed and celebrated as publication took place sequentially in the late 1840s and 1850s. No doubt her inspiration and application came from the peace and tranquillity of the setting, and the panoramic views across Morecambe Bay to the Lakeland fells. Gaskell's novel *Ruth*, published in 1853, is about an orphaned seamstress who catches the eye of a gentleman Henry Bellingham. It compassionately deals with prevailing attitudes to illegitimacy and sin.

The tower itself was built as a 'belvedere' – Italian for beautiful view – for Lancashire banker Henry Paul Fleetwood, who bought the Gibraltar Estate in Silverdale as a country retreat, away from the industrial grime of Preston and Blackburn, where he lived and made his money. How Gaskell came to rent the property as a writing retreat is not known, but she is said to have described the premises as 'an old square tower or Peel (Pele), a remnant of the Border towers', which seems to be a romantic interpretation rather than a factual description.

The inside of the three-storey building, variously known as the Lindeth Tower, Tower House and Gibraltar Tower, has been substantially modernised in recent times, and is now rented out for holidays in the summer and autumn months. The kitchen and bathroom are on the ground floor, the bedroom on the next, and the living room above, topped by an open viewing space. There's an acre of walled garden, and the shelter provided allows cherries and figs to be grown.

Address Lindeth Road, Silverdale, Carnforth, LA5 0TX | **Getting there** Five miles by car from Carnforth to Silverdale; by train to Silverdale station, then walk a mile along Red Bridge Lane, Slackwood Lane, and Lindeth Road | **Hours** Always visible from the road; for hire in summer and autumn | **Tip** Wolf House Gallery, on nearby Lindeth Road, is run by the unusually named artist and illustrator Bells Scambler; it sells original work by British artists and makers, along with hand-picked gifts and homewares (www.wolfhousegallery.com).

26 The Entertainer Theatre

Classical columns lead to a classic film

It was an unexpected stroke of luck when large wooden cladding boards fell off the entrance to Morecambe's once-famous Alhambra Palace Theatre. The boarding had been put up to 'modernise' the building after it closed down in 1970 following a fire. Suddenly, two original, stone-carved, classical columns on each side of the old theatre doorway were revealed, a reminder of the late Victorian, early Edwardian grandeur of the new enterprise, when it opened in 1901. In addition, on the floor were mosaic tiles with the name 'Alhambra' picked out. Now, passers-by on the seafront Marine Road pavement can take it all in, looking across Morecambe's West End Promenade and out to sea.

It might not rival London's famous West End 'Theatreland', but in its day, the popular resort's Alhambra was quite a player. It was something of an irony that John Osborne's celebrated film *The Entertainer* should be shot inside the Alhambra in 1960. Just as Morecambe had its heyday, so Osborne reflected Britain's post-colonial decline, using the mechanism of a fast-fading stage star, Archie Rice, played by Laurence Olivier. The all-star cast included Joan Plowright and Morecambe's very own Thora Hird, born and brought up a short distance away.

Today, brave but practical attempts are well under way to retain and revive the theatre as a retail and entertainment hub, with a balance of volunteers, and professional, revenue-earning initiatives. The ground floor houses a huge fishing shop, the upstairs bar has been reopened, with its magnificent views over the bay, and the Alhambra Live music venue is a stage for touring bands. All these enterprising initiatives are being undertaken in conjunction with the attempts to give new life to the Winter Gardens theatre, and with the hopes and aspirations surrounding the planned Eden Project North, which should be a game-changer for the resort.

Address 56 Marine Road West, Morecambe, LA4 4EU, +44 (0)7771 200873, www.alhambralive.com | **Getting there** 15-minute walk from Morecambe station; bus 2X or 6A | **Hours** The bar with beautiful bay views is open daily noon–10pm | **Tip** Stroll across the road to the seafront West End Gardens, which has some adventurous public sculptures, including *The Hook* – a 10-metre metal sculpture on a fishing theme.

27 Eric Gill Mural

Hero and villain of the Midland Hotel

To art lovers, it can be a 'Staircase to Heaven'; to critics, it's a 'Staircase to Hell'. On one hand, the sculptor, designer and typographer, Eric Gill, was a genius of his age. He was the creator of the beautifully crafted mural which looks down from the ceiling, high above the spiral staircase that greets visitors inside Morecambe's magnificent Art Deco Midland Hotel. On the other hand, to those taking a moral stand, Gill was a self-centred predator who stopped at nothing to gratify his sexual lust. Mistresses might be forgiven: his sisters, daughters and even a pet dog horrified one and all, once the truth was out.

Yet, on the artistic front alone, Gill is still revered for his depiction of relevant classical scenes, to add 'colour' and to break the straight-line simplicity of the 1930s Streamline Moderne style exemplified by the Midland Hotel. Architect Oliver Hill brought in Gill − not knowing of his apparently-insatiable, sexual predilections − to add a classical grandeur to the enterprise. Artistically, it paid off. Gill's 'Neptune and Triton Medallion', seen on high in the open-aspect Staircase Tower, certainly concentrates the mind, and the spiral staircase is wonderful in its own right.

Another Gill artwork is the huge bas-relief behind the reception desk, which has its own controversial story. Provocative and carefree as ever, Gill wanted to depict frolicking nudes, with the title 'High Jinks in Paradise'. Hill asked him to think again, and Gill eventually chose 'Odysseus welcomed from the sea by Nausicaa', which had a suitable marine theme. Gill completed his 'trilogy' with an expansive wall map of North West England in what is the Gill Meeting Room. It remains as an inspiring and thoughtful piece of work. Over the Lake District, he depicts two ethereal lovers flying towards each other. Beautiful and romantic, and tasteful for once.

Address Marine Road West, Morecambe, LA4 4BU, +44 (0)1524 424000, www.englishlakes.co.uk | Getting there 10-minute walk down Central Drive from Morecambe station; by car, exit 34 on M6, following Bay Gateway/A683 to A589 in Morecambe | Hours Open daily | Tip High above the hotel entrance, Gill carved two seahorses that have a shrimp-like appearance, with a nod to Morecambe's classic seafood offering. The car park gate posts are topped with 'Tower of Babel' fixtures, to add to the effect.

28 The Failure's Grave

Epitaph leaves more questions than answers

'Poet, philosopher and failure' – it's not every day you find such words carved clearly at the bottom of a stone-carved memorial. It's certainly intriguing, and begs the question, who would admit to being a failure, and want the words there for posterity, for all to see? This most unexpected of epitaphs can be found on a gravestone in the graveyard of St Peter's Church, on the headland above Heysham Village.

Two Christian names, carved out underneath, say simply *Sarah Hannah*, who was the wife of a James Jones. She died in 1909, at the age of 44. Underneath her name is that of another Sarah, the second wife of James, the inscription telling us that she died in 1929. Then comes the name of James Jones himself, who died a year later, at the age of 91. Yet records show that he was buried in another churchyard several miles away in Morecambe.

So, which one of these three is the poet, philosopher and failure? There is little doubt that it was James Jones, who was quite a character, both in Heysham, and across the Atlantic in America. He spent much of his life in the USA, rubbing shoulders with several American luminaries, including President Ulysses S. Grant, hero of the Unionists as the victorious general in the American Civil War. Jones himself enlisted, and also claimed to have seen President Abraham Lincoln and Harriet Beecher Stowe, author of *Uncle Tom's Cabin*. Jones subsequently worked for Hiram Maxim, inventor of the machine gun, and later on helped to lay out Washington Circle, on Pennsylvania Avenue, near the White House.

Back in Heysham, he became a water inspector, then a Hackney Carriage inspector, although his preferred mode of transport was a tricycle. He wrote poems on a regular basis for a national newspaper, and with all his worldly experience, he must have been quite philosophical. Yet, unaccountably, he felt he had been a failure!

POET
PHILOSOPHER
&
FAILURE

SARAH HANNAH
WIFE OF JAMES JONES
WHO PASSED AWAY
SEP 5TH 1909 AGE LL

SARAH ELIZABETH (SADIE)

WHO DIED NOV 20TH

GUARDIAN ANGELS

JAMES JONES

Address St Peter's Church Graveyard, off Main Street, Heysham, LA3 2RN | Getting there By car, J 34 M 6, then follow the A 683 and A 589 to Main Street, Heysham; bus 2X from Morecambe bus station to Heysham Main Street, or bus 1A to Sugham Lane | Hours Daylight hours | Tip The cover of a Black Sabbath album features six graves from one single slab of sandstone on Heysham Headland. They can be found just above St Peter's Church, and near the ruins of St Patrick's Church. They are at least 1,000 years old, and pre-date the Norman Invasion.

29 Fairy Steps

Wishful thinking on the corpse trail

Kids love the story about the Fairy Steps, but they are told only half a tale. Local legend has it that the fairies in the Slack Head area above Beetham use the narrow, limestone steps as an escape route if in danger. The free spirits are so nimble that they skip up or down them at speed, without touching the sides of the narrow slit between huge slabs of rock. It's said that if a human descends or ascends the steps in similar fashion, the fairies will grant them a wish. In times past, some locals claim they actually witnessed fairies skipping up the steps, though that may be after a few drinks at the nearby Wheatsheaf Inn.

So what is the other half of the story that might take the romance off Beetham's fairy tale? The steps are part of Morecambe Bay's Corpse Trail, along which dead bodies were carried from surrounding villages to be buried at Beetham Church. Iron rings can still be found on rock faces above the Fairy Steps, to help haul up the coffins. Before local churches were built in smaller communities, coffins were even carried over the treacherous sands and channels of Morecambe Bay, en route for Beetham.

For today's visitors, the short walk is not difficult, although you have to watch your step on the uneven and pitted limestone surfaces, and the path above and below can be muddy after rainy spells. It's a fine experience for all the family, and can be quite a fun outing. In the woodland area are the first hints of fairy activity, with decorations and mementoes hanging on trees and bushes. Painted stones can often be seen, and even small fairy doors that they have left behind for your entertainment. It's all part of the fairy folklore in these parts, with stories of caves stacked with gold on which fairies are said to dance. But even if the spirits don't grant you any wish, you couldn't wish for better views. En route, two tree stumps fascinate – one with a direction finder on top, the other with coins hammered in.

Address Fairy Steps, Milnthorpe, Carnforth, LA7 7BD | **Getting there** By car, A6 northbound from M6 J35, turn off at Beetham and head up towards Slack Head; turn right on to Leighton Road and Highcote Lane, where the path leads to the Fairy Steps | **Hours** Always accessible | **Tip** Visit the beautiful, Grade I-listed St Michael and All Angels Church at Beetham, with its long, flower-decked archway entrance, take tea at the Old Beetham Post Office and Tea Room, or have a fine meal at the Wheatsheaf.

30 Far Arnside Tower

Beware the Border Reivers

It's hard to imagine nowadays, but the areas to the north and west of Carnforth once lived in constant fear of attack by fearsome raiders from Scotland, all of 70 miles away. Sir Walter Scott called them the 'Border Reivers', brigands who crossed the Scottish border and came south to plunder vulnerable farmsteads in England's Northern counties. Not that it was one-way traffic: the English could be just as bad in going north to do the same. Yet it is something of a surprise when you look out from the Arnside to Silverdale road and catch sight of the seemingly impregnable, five-storey mini castle-like structure known as Arnside Tower.

The thickly-walled building is typical of the fortified farmhouses in the area, an example being the one just south of Beetham, on the present A6. They were called Peel, or Pele Towers and were usually three storeys high, the bottom tier being the stockade for the cattle that were brought in during sieges. It's not surprising that they were built when you consider the state of lawlessness that stalked the northern lands between the 13th and 17th centuries. Tensions were constantly high between the Scots and the English, and authority was weak in these remote areas.

Arnside Tower was built by the De Broughton family around 1340, but changed hands over the centuries. It was rebuilt in 1464 by Lord Hastings, and its design is said to be based on his castle at Ashby de la Zouch in Leicestershire. It was repaired after a serious fire in 1602, and was in use defensively until the end of the 17th century. Its last inhabitants were a William Coward and his sister Agnes Wheeler, an 18th-century dialect writer. A wall collapsed around 1900 and though the building is in a ruinous state, it remains a Scheduled Monument, with Grade II-listed status. A public footpath runs alongside, but the public are warned not to go inside. Ironically, cattle kept on nearby upland pastures are Scottish Highland.

Address Near Arnside Tower Farm, Far Arnside, LA5 0SN | Getting there From Silverdale, just three minutes by car on Cove Road towards Arnside | Hours Always accessible | Tip The Bowk Stone is a huge, round and highly-fissured lump of limestone, transported by a glacier and deposited near Challan Hall, in Silverdale, on the road from Beetham. Legend has it that a serpent coiled round the stone, waiting to snatch passing sheep, before dragging its victims into nearby Hawes Water.

31 *Fireworks and Flags* Mural
Wet and wild at the Midland Hotel

The flamboyant and fun *Fireworks and Flags* mural in the Midland Hotel's stunning Rotunda Bar is a clear case of 'third time lucky'. The original commission in the 1930s drove renowned artist Eric Ravilious and his wife Tirzah to distraction. When they arrived to put paint to their ideas during the inclement summer of 1933, they found that the wall plaster was still wet, and with no white paint finish for them to work on.

Delay after delay blighted their efforts, and when the painters warned the work's commissioners that the mural would not last, they were told the most important thing was to have it finished by opening day, regardless of its durability. Understandably, this outraged their artistic sensibility, not to mention the ultimate futility of the task in hand. However, the couple pressed on with their creation, which depicted a fireworks display over the pier and the surrounding sea in the vast expanse of Morecambe Bay. They duly finished their artwork in time for the prestigious opening.

Despite remedial work after the opening, the mural duly deteriorated and eventually fell apart. Fifty or so years later, when ITV filmed several *Poirot* scenes at the Midland in the 1980s, and with David Suchet due to grace the hotel for several key shoots, designers created a replacement to give the place more authenticity. They were true to the original Art Deco-style mural, although even this new artwork deteriorated over time.

Move on to 2013 when the then-crumbling hotel was refurbished by Manchester's Urban Splash company, and two murals were commissioned, based on the original Ravilious drawings and designs. Today, this is what delights the visitor to the Rotunda Bar, which is a sheer delight in itself. The iconic mural designs, the illuminated crystal centrepiece, and the views out to sea give a taste of those far-off days of 1930s style.

Address Marine Road West, Morecambe, LA4 4BU, +44 (0)1524 424000, www.englishlakes.co.uk | Getting there By car, exit 34 on M6, following Bay Gateway / A683 to A589 in Morecambe, turn left on Marine Road, 10-minute walk down Central Drive from station | Hours Open daily | Tip Lunch in the Ravilious Bar and savour the mural, illuminated by the purple-lit chandelier over the bar, plus the panoramic sea views.

32 Galgate Silk Mill
Revolution and rhubarb go in the pot

Galgate's Silk Mill, still standing proud today, traces its history back to the 18th century. Yet it was revolutionary in its activities when it ultimately got up steam. Originally, little Galgate, located just south of Lancaster itself, boasted a water-driven corn mill on the River Conder, right up until 1792. It was then that a spinning mill for waste silk was set up, reputedly the first mechanical silk mill in the entire country.

With Britain's Industrial Revolution rapidly beginning to take shape, inventions and ingenuity added to the mill's capacity. By 1832, two huge beam engines were installed alongside a new boiler and engine house, complete with square chimney. The mill remained independent for well over a hundred years, when the business was acquired by leading textile firm Paton and Baldwins, only closing down in 1971.

Today, the historic silk mill is now a mixture of small industrial units and a well-appreciated café. But one of the claimed legacies of the silk spinning industry is the growing of rhubarb in the town. It's thought that the profusion of rhubarb was its usefulness for making a dye for the silk. As such, plenty of gardeners and those with allotments grew rhubarb in abundance, and, to an extent, the tradition lives on. With a sense of humour, Galgate's local community newsletter is called 'Rhubarb City News', the term 'rhubarb, rhubarb', being a phrase traditionally used by comedians to indicate crowd noises or indistinct conversation at best.

Local resident and celebrity gardener Fred Downham helped cement the name 'Rhubarb City', well before he passed away in 2020, aged 91. During his time as a regular expert on BBC Radio 4's *Gardeners' Question Time*, he highlighted the fact that his home town grew the tasty vegetable in abundance, and that the local newsletter had been given its name in honour of the fact.

Address Silk Mill Café, Chapel Lane, Galgate, LA2 0PR | Getting there By car, M 6 J 33, then A 6 north; busses are at least twice hourly from Lancaster station: 41 (Preston) or 42 (Garstang) | Hours Café open Mon–Fri 8.30am–2pm, Sat 9am–1.30pm | Tip Galgate Marina on the Lancaster Canal is well equipped for residents, leisure, visitor and winter moorings; narrow boats can be hired and The Plough public house is two minutes away (www.aqua vista.com).

33__GB Antiques Centre

Cornucopia of collectables and curios

It's quite something to crow about: in an era when antiques are all the rage, Lancaster has what is claimed to be the largest indoor antiques and furniture centre in the country. Each year, the family-owned GB Antiques Centre attracts around 220,000 visitors, who either buy from or trade with the 120 dealers as they pack into the vast area, spread out over a single floor. It's a vintage Heaven for those fascinated by the traditional. Even without any retail therapy in mind, it's a magnificent sight, with things of beauty and fascination all around.

The 'GB' behind its name is not that of Great Britain, but the initials of Gloria Blackburn, who opened the centre with her husband Allan in 1990. Initially, the plan was to open at weekends only, with occasional antique fairs into the bargain. However, the Blackburns quickly realised that interest and demand was sufficient to open more often. Now, the centre is open every day, except Christmas and Boxing Day.

Virtually everything imaginable is here, from pottery to paintings to porcelain, glassware to clocks, furniture to fine art, and dolls to decorations. Items are well displayed so the observer can appreciate their beauty, originality and craftsmanship. Preservation and heritage are a given, with furniture fashioned from Georgian mahogany, Victorian pine and Edwardian oak. Each dealer has their own specialism, such as antique furniture, kitchen and glassware, pottery, toys, or sundry memorabilia.

The centre is just one part of Lancaster Leisure Park, which hosts Lancaster Brewery, a farm shop, a factory outlet, home-grown garden plots, and a children's adventure play zone. The range of attractions on offer also include a farm shop, a factory shop, an ice cream parlour, a portrait photography studio, a dance studio, a countryside kitchen and the City of Lancaster Gymnastics centre.

Address Lancaster Leisure Park, Wyresdale Road, Lancaster, LA1 3LA | Getting there
Bus 18 is infrequent but direct from Lancaster bus station; bus 89 passes nearby; by car,
from M6 J33 take the A6 north | Hours Daily 10am–5pm | Tip For rest and relaxation,
the leisure park has a Forest Garden, two acres of woodland and wildlife habitat areas, with
pathways through it.

34 George Fox Bust
Jail Hell Hole for the Quaker maker

The steely look on the face of George Fox's bust in Lancaster Castle says it all. Staring out of a glass-fronted recess in the courtyard, his determined countenance has been captured perfectly by sculptor Alan Ward, who works in the castle's sculpture workshop. And the founder of the Quaker sect, which broke away from established religious practices, needed all his resolve after he was arrested for blasphemy, and incarcerated in Lancaster Castle's cells.

He called it 'The Dark House', a Hell hole that let in the rain, the wind and the cold. At his trial, he insisted the judge see the conditions for himself before being found guilty. Eventually, an influential supporter appealed directly to the restored monarch, Charles II, and Fox was released.

Despite his persecution, Fox's spiritual influence cannot be denied. In the mid-17th century, he rooted the new Quaker religion throughout the old counties of Lancashire and Westmorland, starting with his 'blinding light vision' on the crest of Pendle Hill, above Clitheroe. There, he had his vision of 'a people in white raiments, waiting to be gathered'.

Fifty miles north, Fox came across a great throng of people dressed in un-dyed white clothes, massed together on the slopes of Firbank Fell, on the Yorkshire-Westmorland border. It was a hiring fair for textile dyers and bleachers, waiting for employers to take them on. Their own work clothes were un-dyed, because it was a waste of time, effort and materials. But to Fox, it was proof of his vision, and he didn't miss the opportunity: his three-hour sermon on a rocky outcrop, now known as Fox's Pulpit, did the trick. Fortuitously, many of the crowd were disillusioned by the whole panoply of the established religion. It was fertile ground for Fox's message of a simple religion that offered a personal relationship with God. He is still revered to this day.

Hand made
in the
Sculpture Workshop
Lancaster Castle
by
Alan Ward

Address Lancaster Castle, Castle Parade, LA1 1YJ | Getting there Three-minute walk from Lancaster railway station or five-minute walk from Lancaster bus station; by car, along the old A6, turn right at Meeting House Lane | Hours Courtyard access: daily 9.30am–5pm | Tip Swarthmore Hall, near Ulverston, is a modern-day Quaker retreat and teaching centre; it was where Fox was sheltered when Quakerism was founded, and remains the religion's spiritual home.

35 George Washington Church

Coat of arms inspires USA's Stars & Stripes

It seems odd to many that every American Independence Day, on 4 July, the Stars and Stripes flag should fly from the tower of St Oswald's Church in the small Lancashire village of Warton, near Carnforth. It's in honour of the USA's first President, George Washington, whose family can be traced back to Warton in the 15th century. But the family's link with the Stars and Stripes flag is even more remarkable. It's claimed that seamstress Betsy Ross, who sewed together the very first Stars and Stripes, did so from a rough-and-ready pencil drawing handed to her by no less than George Washington himself – and his sketch copied the armorial bearings of the Washington family's coat of arms. This had three red stars and two red stripes on a white background. For 'stars' read 'mullets', and for 'stripes' read 'bars', to use the proper terminology – but the significance is not lost.

For proof of the Warton connection with the Washington family, visitors to St Oswald's Church can still see the stone-carved coat of arms that is now on the inside wall of St Oswald's sturdy tower, which was built by Washington's philanthropic ancestor, Robert, more than 500 years ago. Originally, the shield was on the outside wall of the tower, but after centuries of erosion threatened its integrity, it was moved inside and had a protective glass cover put over it in 1955.

George Washington's English connections are mostly associated with Sulgrave Manor, north of Oxford, and his ancestor John, who left for America in 1657, with George being born in Virginia in 1732. However, the family can be traced back to County Durham, from where Robert Washington left to settle near Kendal in old Westmorland, while owning land in the Warton area to the south. Naturally, the nearby pub and hotel in Warton is called the George Washington, with American visitors beating a path to its door.

Address Main Street, Warton, Carnforth, LA5 9PG, +44 (0)1524 732946, www.ubwby.org | **Getting there** Five minutes by car from Carnforth railway station or a half-hour walk | **Hours** See website for current information on visiting | **Tip** Another connection with the Washington family is in St Martin's Church in Bowness-on-Windermere, where a stained-glass window contains the family coat of arms; George's ancestor, John, died in Bowness in 1407.

36_ Ghost of the Marsh
Bridal apparition that haunts Bolton-le-Sands

Walkers on the coastal path at Bolton-le-Sands, between Morecambe and Carnforth, are warned about potentially-treacherous gulleys, the deadly quicksands of Morecambe Bay, and the tide that can come in 'faster than a galloping horse'. Which one of these claimed the life of a local bride on the day of her marriage, we will never know. However, there are many reports of her weeping and wailing apparition being sighted to this day, as she walks the lonely marshes, pulling up the fringe of her wedding dress to keep it out of the mud. We also know why the distraught bride – known locally either as 'The Grey Lady', or by her real name of Matilda – took her own life on what should have been her happiest day.

The truth is that the local Lord of the Manor, Giles de Bois, summoned Matilda to his home on the eve of her wedding, and there claimed the archaic right of 'first night' – sleeping with common women before they wed. The next day, the distraught young woman put on her wedding dress and walked across the marshes towards the sea to drown. Her fiancé vowed revenge, and hired an assassin by the name of 'Black Betty'. Although this was achieved and the Lord of the Manor was slaughtered, Matilda's spirit remains on the marshes, unable to find her peace. Her restless spirit has even been felt, and the apparition seen, on the banks of the nearby Lancaster Canal, which runs parallel to the coast at Bolton-le-Sands.

The main sightings of 'The Grey Lady' have been along the stretches of tidal marshland between Red Bank Farm and Mill Lane, which leads to the village of Bolton-le-Sands. Nearby, along the cliffs towards Morecambe, is the monument to the tragedy of the Chinese cocklers, but that's another story (see ch. 74). More joyfully, the sights and sounds of the flocks of seabirds, both onshore and on the sand spits in the bay, create a truly uplifting experience.

Address Coastal marshes off Red Bank Farm, LA5 8JR | **Getting there** By car, from Morecambe, take the Coastal Road north to Bolton-le-Sands; turn left into Pasture Lane to the coast and the farm | **Tip** A four-mile circular walk from Bay View Garden Centre, Bolton-le-Sands, starts up Mill Lane to Lancaster Canal, then south to the Hest Bank Hotel, back down to the coast, then north to Red Bank Farm, and on to the garden centre, with its lovely café (www.archers-redbankfarm.co.uk).

37 __ Gillows at Leighton Hall

Please touch the furniture!

The Georgian elegance of Gillow furniture kept Lancaster on the map. Sadly, much of the funding and raw materials were based on the slave trade. And as you look at some of the finest pieces of Gillow craftsmanship in the family-owned Leighton Hall, near Carnforth, or Lancaster's Judges' Lodgings, it's hard to forget the connection. Not that this uncomfortable history detracts from the skills and endeavours brought to the tables, chairs and cabinets fashioned by founder Robert Gillow from 1728 onwards. For over 200 years, the Gillow brand was up there with the names of Chippendale, Hepplewhite and Sheraton.

The Gillow Furniture Gallery in the Judges' Lodgings follows the growth and importance of the firm, and each of the furnished rooms displays the range of the firm's Lancaster craftsmen. The Gillow offices and workshops are across the road at the side of Castle Hill, and though there is a plaque outside, the building is now privately owned and no access is possible. Leighton Hall, bought by Robert's grandson Richard from a cousin in 1822, and still partly occupied by the Gillow family, is a magnificent stately home, now divided into apartments. Unusually, and unstuffily, when you visit, you may look close up at the Gillow furniture, and even play the Steinway piano!

Over the centuries, Gillows has had several mergers and takeovers, but the Georgian period still looms large in its history. Founder Robert was the joiner turned furniture-maker who built the firm, funded by his part-ownership in a ship that plied the triangular slavery trade route between Lancaster, West Africa and the Caribbean. On its final leg, back to the River Lune, the vessel brought the mahogany, rum and sugar that made fortunes for Robert and his partners. His connections with fellow Catholics in North Lancashire gave him access to the gentry, and thus a ready-made market.

Address Leighton Hall, Storrs Lane, Yealand Conyers, Carnforth, LA5 9ST | Getting there By car, from M6 J35, follow Carnforth signs to Roundabout, north on the A6, then brown signs for Leighton Hall | **Hours** Traditionally early May to late September 2–5pm | Tip Why not factor in a stroll along the nearby Woodland Garden Path, taking in the walled garden, the path maze, bee corner, a bird of prey display, adventure playground and the Tree Face Trail for children.

38 Gillow's Mausoleum
Design for the dead

It's a family mausoleum that makes quite a statement. Maybe what you might expect from the Gillows, the celebrated furniture makers in Lancaster, and a leading Catholic family in North Lancashire. But the size, design, style and location still provide a shock. It's in the middle of nowhere, almost buried in the midst of a tranquil wood half a mile from Thurnham Hall, and five miles south of Lancaster. It's a huge sandstone oblong, and on each side has four Egyptian columns, recessed under the roof.

Equally surprising is the Catholic church next to the mausoleum: the Church of St Thomas and Elizabeth is much larger than you might expect for such a rural and relatively sparsely populated area, which runs to the coast in the west and the River Lune estuary in the north. Having said that, who would expect to find a fully-fledged Catholic monastery, in the shape of Cockersands Abbey, on the very edge of the sea, and now in ruins since the Dissolution of 1539. Its octagonal Chapter House survived because it was used as a burial chamber for the resident family at Thurnham Hall. Three prominent families – all landowners in the area – paid for the building of the church. Firstly, the Gillows, who had homes in nearby Forton, and later at Leighton Hall, near Carnforth; John Dalton, whose family supported the Jacobite Rebellion of 1715, and who lived in Thurnham Hall; and Richard Worswick, the family of Lancaster bankers.

The Grade II-listed mausoleum is said to have been designed by Robert Gillow, though it is claimed to be similar to that found at Temple Mills in Leeds. It was finished in 1830, by which time three generations of Gillows had run the family's high-quality furniture-making firm in Lancaster's Castle Street. Back in 1814, the firm was taken over but continued with the name Gillow, which had become a byword for quality and style.

Address St Thomas and St Elizabeth Catholic Church, Lodge Cottages, LA2 0DT |
Getting there By car, from Lancaster, take the Ashton Road/A 588 to Thurnham Hall |
Hours Always accessible | Tip The Grade II-listed Anglican Christ Church at nearby
Glasson has an east window containing stained-glass made by the celebrated Lancaster
specialists Shrigley and Hunt (www.christchurchglasson.com).

39 __ Glasson Dock

The port that saved the Lune

Glasson Dock, billed as 'the port that saved the Lune', is a major surprise for many. Visitors to the area south of the river, near to the point where it enters Morecambe Bay, don't expect to see a fully-functioning dock and large adjacent marina in a rural setting just five miles from the centre of Lancaster. Glasson is also quite a tourist delight in its own right too, with its indoor and outdoor cafés affording views of the dock and marina, and the single-track, swing bridge in-between. The marina is home to pleasure boats of all shapes and sizes, whereas the dock, known as the Port of Lancaster, deals mainly with coal, foodstuffs and fertiliser. There's much speculation about the name 'Glasson': some says it's Cornish for 'glazier' or 'glass blower', others claim it's a shortened version of the Scottish 'McGlasson', or even the French 'glacé', for cold. Take your pick.

As ships increased in size and draught, Lancaster was left high and dry for ocean-going merchant ships as the 18th century progressed. And when Sunderland Point on the north bank was outgrown, the radical solution was to build a proper, tidal-locked basin for larger vessels. The desire to keep a port for Lancaster was certainly there, as first the dock was built in 1782, then a link to the Lancaster Canal at Galgate some time later, followed by a five-mile railway branch line to Lancaster alongside the River Lune. Though long closed, it remains a walking and cycling route as part of the Lancashire Greenway.

A limited amount of commercial traffic still uses the dock, with outbound shipments including coal for the Isle of Man and the Western Isles of Scotland. Incoming cargoes include animal feed and fertiliser, which are stored in large sheds on the dock side. River traffic is limited, due to the shallow nature of the River Lune, with the window of access being limited to high tide. In its heyday, up to 25 ships could be in the dock at one time.

Address Glasson Dock, LA2 0BT | **Getting there** By car, from A6, take Ashton Road, then follow signs for Glasson at Condor Green; bus 89 to Knott End from George Street in Lancaster; on foot or bicycle, take the Lune Estuary Footpath for a near-two-hour walk | **Hours** Always accessible | **Tip** There are a couple of good cafés at Glasson, but if you wish to stay and dine in the area, the characterful Mill at Conder Green, a few minutes from Glasson and 15 minutes from Lancaster, is a good option.

40　The Golden Lion

A tipple before a topple

The Golden Lion in Lancaster is a pub with a difference. It's en route from the cells of Lancaster Castle to Gallow's Hill, and the traditional 'boozer' was the place where those condemned to die by the rope could have their last drink on this Earth. By tradition, prisoners would sit on their own coffins on the back of a horse-drawn cart, which would take them up Moor Lane towards the place on the edge of Lancaster Moor where the hangman awaited.

As you stand in the bar in the Golden Lion, it's an eerie feeling to be exactly where hundreds of condemned prisoners were allowed time for a last drink. Apparently, one man sent to hang didn't drink alcoholic beverages, so he was sent straight to his death from prison. Little did he know that his appeal against hanging was granted, but the horseman bringing the message arrived just a minute or two too late. If the victim had taken a drink at the Golden Lion, his life would have been spared.

The pub is also on the official Pendle Witch Trail that stretches between Lancaster Castle Jail and East Lancashire's Pendle Hill, where the so-called witches lived in surrounding villages. Much is made of the trials in Lancaster and Pendle's history, with events being held to mark the 400th anniversary in 2012. The trial is one of the most famous in English history: in a time of superstition and fear, everything was put at the door of so-called witches, who were often loners or eccentrics. It could be the death of a child, or even a horse, the causing of lameness or sickness.

In all, 10 people were hanged on 12 August, 1612, and all passed through the Golden Lion on their way to the gallows. Today, the pub is regarded as one of the best traditional pubs in Lancaster. It's a place of conviviality and warmth, with its roaring open fire and a wide range of cask ales on offer, both national and local. With live DJs and an open mic night, it's a lively place.

Address 33 Moor Lane, Lancaster, LA1 1QD, +44 (0)1524 842198 | Getting there Five-minute walk from Lancaster bus station or 10-minute walk from the railway station; by car, from M6 J34, follow signs to Lancaster, then take the A6 through Lancaster | Hours Daily 2pm–midnight, open later Fri & Sat | Tip Another traditional pub is the Pendle Witch in Penny Street, which serves good beer and food, and has a beer garden too.

41__Greenway Cycle Route
Pedal power in Morecambe and Lancaster

On Morecambe Promenade, just west of the Midland Hotel, is a special junction for cyclists, where two significant cycle paths meet. To the north is the coast-hugging 'Bay Cycle Way', while going inland is the 'Way of the Roses', stretching all the way from coast to coast. Both routes share the Lancaster-Morecambe Greenway section from Morecambe Promenade to Lancaster, a three-mile route on the former, direct railway line to the River Lune crossing point on Lancaster's stylish Millennium Bridge. This was designed for cyclists and pedestrians only and is known locally as the 'V-sign Bridge' due to its giant steel structure in the shape of a letter 'V' (see ch. 106). But rather than telling you to go away, it's a welcoming sight for all.

The Greenway, and the Morecambe Promenade section, both show a touch of genius – environmentally, ecologically, and in terms of encouraging traffic-free appreciation of the magnificent Bay scenery, with its 20-square miles of ever-changing channels, shifting sands, shining seas and amazing sunsets.

Thousands of locals and visitors use the Greenway, which links three of the area's major supermarkets. Popping in for provisions is positively encouraged: ideal for cycling commuters and self-cooking Airbnb vacationers. Visitors can savour Lancaster's Roman and Georgian splendour before linking up with the stunning views of Morecambe Bay and the distant views of the Lakeland fells and mountains across the glistening waters. With fresh air in their lungs, cyclists can take in the Victorian and Edwardian features of the old resort, not to mention the 1930s Art Deco, Streamline Moderne-style Midland Hotel, shaped like a ship in its seafront setting.

The five-mile long, stone-built Promenade was built on the back of a Government sea-defence grant, another touch of genius to revive and refresh the old resort.

Address Near Midland Hotel, Morecambe, LA4 4BU | Getting there The signpost point where the two routes combine is on Morecambe seafront where Central Drive meets Marine Road Central, adjacent to the Midland Hotel | Hours All year-round | Tip Take a small diversion from the Lancaster Canal north of Bolton-le-Sands down to the A6 (Main Road). Turn left down Mill Lane, over the railway bridge to Bay View Garden Centre and Restaurant, LA5 8ET. Great views out to sea, great variety of plants, and excellent food.

42___The Hanging Corner

Stepping through the window of death

An elegant French window in a perfectly-proportioned small round tower has a sinister and deadly past. The tower at Lancaster Castle is called 'The Hanging Corner' – the setting for more than 200 executions between 1800 and 1865. It's said that more prisoners were sentenced to death at Lancaster Castle's Assize Court (see ch. 20) than any other place outside London. The French window would open, and the condemned prisoner stepped out on to a temporarily-erected scaffold, erected the previous day.

Perhaps just as shocking was the fact that the prisoner would face a crowd of between 5,000 and 6,000 people, who had assembled on the grassy bank opposite: the act of death was a public spectacle, until a change in the law prohibited such events in 1868. Thereafter, hangings were carried out inside the castle, next to the chapel – presumably for a last act of forgiveness to be administered before the trapdoor opened.

Prior to 1800, all executions for the county of Lancashire took place on Gallows Hill, on the moors outside Lancaster's southern gate, a place that is now inside the town's lofty Williamson's Park. One of the most notorious hanging episodes was that of the Pendle Witches in 1612. In the Forest of Pendle area, near the towns of Nelson and Colne, the so-called witches were accused of causing the deaths of 17 people. There were also claims of them plotting to blow up Lancaster Castle. The evidence was thin or non-existent, but 9 of the 10 who were found guilty were hanged on Gallows Hill, the other in York.

Today, visitors to Lancaster Castle can take in the relics and artefacts of the period in the appropriately-named 'Drop Room' on the bottom floor. From 1900 onwards, a purpose-built execution shed was used for hangings, and though the barbarism continued in private, it would never surpass the record number of 20 people despatched in 1817.

Address Castle Grove, LA1 1YN | **Getting there** A three-minute walk from Lancaster station | **Hours** Daily 9.30am–5pm; inside tours must be booked | **Tip** Keep your eyes peeled, and your senses alert, for the ghost of a monk with a noose round his neck, or the spectre of Pendle witch, Elizabeth Southerns – just two of the ghostly presences that are said to wander the castle and its courtyard.

43　Hark to Bounty Inn

Howling dog inspires pub's unusual name

It's not every day you find a pub that's named after a howling dog! But the 'Hark to Bounty' is just that, and the story behind its unusual name is equally intriguing. Back in 1875, the local hunt in the Ribble Valley village of Slaidburn, just north of Clitheroe, was mustering outside the local pub, when the leader of the hunt called for a drinks break, with the whole retinue joining him. The local squire, also the village parson, was a member of the hunt, and had a dog called Bounty, who was left outside along with the other dogs of the pack. The dogs wanted to get on the trail and began howling loudly. Above the din could be heard one dog in particular – the one owned by the squire. As the group listened, the squire exclaimed: 'Hark to Bounty!' – and the name caught on. From that day forward, the pub was referred to by its new title, and its name was soon changed for good, from its previous and rather unadventurous moniker of 'The Dog'.

The pub itself is a fascinating building, and even has its own incorporated courthouse, which can still be visited. The old Manorial or Moot Court – complete with its characterful, A-frame oak roof – dealt with local issues such as land transactions and disputes, and the punishment of local miscreants. The first-floor courtroom is accessed by stone steps on the outside of the building: it literally held court from the 19th century right up until 1937, and now acts as a one-of-a-kind function room. The pub building dates back to the 1300s, and functioned as a coaching inn from the 16th century onwards.

Today, it continues as a traditional country pub, but is also residential, with a restaurant, lounge, and sauna. It has also appeared in *The Good Pub Guide* for five consecutive years. The area is excellent walking country, on both Pendle Hill and in the Forest of Bowland Area of Outstanding Natural Beauty.

Address Town End, Slaidburn, Clitheroe, BB7 3EP | Getting there Bus 628 from Clitheroe railway station; by car, from Lancaster railway station via Wyresdale Road, across the Trough of Bowland pass and on to Slaidburn | Hours Thu–Sun 8am–11pm | Tip Take in the fine wine and spirits shop, D. Byrne and Co, in King Street, Clitheroe, beneath which are a series of catacombs containing thousands of bottles from all over the world.

44 The Headless Lady

Grave concern over woman who beat the clock

It's a sight for sore eyes: if only the headless lady, laid out on top of the tomb, actually had any. There she lies, languishing on the tomb's once-white marble chest in the tranquil churchyard of Lancaster Priory. Was she beheaded? Or did her head simply fall off – along with the end of her right arm? Probably the latter: after all, she has held this reclining pose for at least 170 years.

So who was the mystery woman? The inscription on her tomb is now well worn, and her carved name is unable to be deciphered. Yet stories about the 'White Lady' abound. She is said to be Ann Rothwell, first wife of Liverpool merchant William Talbot Rothwell, who lived at Ellel, a village just south of Lancaster. The effigy is quite a curiosity for visitors to the churchyard, which can be found behind Lancaster Castle (see ch. 20), and the story behind her demise certainly adds to the drama. Legend has it that she fell to her death from the Priory Church bell tower, while attempting to turn back the hands of the clock in an effort to buy time, and potentially save her lover from a 'high noon' execution at the adjacent castle. As is the way with hand-me-down tales, however, it's unclear whether Ann was pushed or jumped. Yet another variation is that she was trying to save her husband, who faced the gallows. The final suggestion is that she was cleaning the clock when she fell to her death. This would seem most unlikely, but to add to the speculation that it could have been foul play, Ann Rothwell did leave a full will and testament.

Naturally, there are claims of a ghostly white lady being seen among the gravestones, and alleged sightings of a white face looking down from the bell tower. And what of her head? Lancaster Priory has it in safe keeping. A fund-raising bid to return it was unsuccessful, so Ann remains headless, if not clueless. Reputedly, Ann can be seen wandering the churchyard at dawn and dusk.

Address Priory Close, Lancaster, LA1 1YZ | Getting there Eight-minute walk from
Lancaster station; by car, coming into Lancaster on A6 | Hours Daily 9.15am–4pm | Tip
The Grade I-listed Priory Church, with its impressive vaulted roof, dates back to 1094. An
Anglo-Saxon Runic Cross found in the churchyard is now in the British Museum.

45   Heron Corn Mill

Water power that goes with the grain

There's something rather wholesome about the milling of flour and the making of good bread. It's even more fulfilling to see it done in traditional fashion, with all the sights and sounds that stretch back to a bygone era. The Heron Corn Mill in the village of Beetham – just over the Lancashire-Cumbria border, and a mere 15 miles from Lancaster – is the perfect example of a working, water-driven corn mill. It was built in 1740, but on a site where milling had been performed since 1096, just 30 years after the Norman invasion.

Present-day millwright Stuart Hobbs still plies his trade at Beetham, milling organic wheat and heritage grains that are naturally more disease resistant, and which are available to buy in the attached Heron Barn. Changes may have occurred over time, but the mill is as it was back in 1850, and holds public demonstrations on the first Friday of the month. The mill was still working commercially until 1952, when animal feeds company W. and J. Pye ended operations there. It was bought and restored by the Beetham Trust, and opened to the public as a heritage centre in 1975. As well as being open to visitors, the mill acts as the local community hub, with the 'Bread of Heron' group meeting weekly. Naturally, baking sessions are on the agenda, and the local theatre group 'Thresh and Ply' puts on regular performances.

In 2007, the mill was serviced by a traditional millwright from Devon, and has since been milling wheat, rye and spelt flour, and hosting tours and demonstrations. It is masterminded by Stuart, who helps with conservation. The mill works by taking water through a sluice gate at the top of the natural weir on the River Bela, funnelling it into a channel called a launder, through which it rushes to power the water wheel. More recently, a hydro-electric turbine has been built to perfect the generation of power required. The mill is a rare example of combining traditional and modern technology.

Address Mill Lane, Beetham, Milnthorpe, LA7 7PQ, +44 (0)1539 564 271, www.heronmill.org | Getting there By car, M6 J35, then follow the A6 north to Beetham, where the corn mill is signposted | Hours Wed–Sun 11am–4pm | Tip The appropriately named Wheatsheaf pub, hotel and restaurant, just round the corner, is a perfect base from which to experience the area.

46 Heysham Nature Reserve
Nurturing nature next to the nukes

You might not expect to find a nature reserve next door to a busy port and dockland (see ch. 47), let alone a nuclear power station. Yet Heysham Nature Reserve can be found just a stone's throw from both – and the three-hectare site boasts a stunning variety of birds, bees and butterflies, and even the great-crested newt. It combines a rich habitat that includes wetlands and reed beds, grasslands and woodlands. Little wonder that in spring and summer the sound of birdsong is an orchestra of avian melodies.

Before we even touch on the rare visitors to the reserve, there are sedge warblers, white throats, meadow pipits, greenfinches, linnets, grasshopper warblers and chiffchaffs, which help make up the birdsong choir. In winter, the visitor can see snipe and water rails, with woodcock frequenting the water's edge. Then there are the migrant birds that congregate on the fringes of the vast Morecambe Bay, which covers no less than 120 square miles of tidal seawater, sea-washed salt marshes, sandbars and ever-changing rivers that flow down from the Cumbrian fells, the Lake District mountains, and the Lancashire moorlands.

The peak times for spotting and ringing of migrant fliers is April and May. On occasions, rare visitors touch down. Over the years, there have been sightings of the wryneck, night heron, serin, woodchat shrike and the yellow-browned warbler, all the way from Siberia. There is a fascinating variety of shrubs and flowers, including the dainty bee orchid, and a host of butterflies, moths and no less than 14 species of dragonfly, including the Emperor. There is on-site parking and several good footpaths and walking trails. Although no dogs are allowed, there is an adjacent dog-friendly area. With all this immersive wildlife, it's easy to forget Heysham's industrial surrounds, in an environment where nuclear and nature coexist side by side.

Address LA3 2XA | Getting there From Heysham Port station and the Ferry Passenger Terminal, a three-minute walk along Princess Alexander Way, turning right into Money Lane; by car, from Heysham Village, via Middleton Way/the A 589 and A 693 | Tip Back in Heysham Village's Main Street, you can snack up at Tracy's Homemade Pies and Cakes.

47 Heysham Port

Roll up, roll-on, roll-off for Klondike Gold Rush

In the middle of winter it's not hard to see why they called Heysham Port's temporary construction villages 'Klondike' and 'Dawson City'. The rows of wooden homes housed hundreds of navvies – the old term for labourers – to build the railway to Heysham, and to dig out the new, deep-water port between 1898 and 1904, when it opened for business. Workers, and sometimes their families too, flocked in to follow the action, just like Alaska's Klondike Gold Rush a couple of years earlier. Today, none of the huts remain, though you can see mound marks at the back of modern-day Heysham Golf Club, marking the spot where 'Klondyke Village' once stood. It may have been rudimentary accommodation, but there was a hotel, a bakery that made 600 loaves a day, a barber shop, a clothing store, a canteen, and even a police station.

If that was the story of old Heysham, it gave rise to modern Heysham, an invention of the Midland Railway, that was behind both the rail and sea development that still thrives today, with ferry services to Northern Ireland, Dublin and the Isle of Man. Ferries covering the route to Douglas operate through the quaintly-named Isle of Man Steam Packet Company. Changes have been made over the years since 1904, with the boom in road transport and containerisation, and the advent of roll-on, roll-off services. However, foot passengers can still arrive by train at Heysham Port Station. The old Midland Railway Company became part of the London, Midland and Scottish back in 1922, and the advent of British Rail followed nationalisation in the late 1940s, until modern-day privatisation.

It's a constantly evolving story, all well chronicled and illustrated by Heysham Heritage Association (see ch. 61), which has an impressive display and an information centre on Main Street in Heysham Village itself. Well worth a visit and a chat with the volunteers. One timeless feature is the original South Pier cast-iron lighthouse.

Address South Quay, Heysham, LA3 2XE | Getting there By car, M6 J34, then follow Bay Gateway signs to Heysham | Hours If using the ferries, 9am–5pm, 10.30pm–2.30am | Tip For excellent breakfasts and lunches, cheerful staff and sea views of the bay and the old harbour lighthouse, try the nearby Half Moon Bay Café (www.halfmoonbaycafe.co.uk).

48 Inn at Whitewell

Home of the Queen's favourite pub lunch

One problem being the Queen is that you can't just pop down to the local for a drink... unless it's the Inn at Whitewell. Her Majesty was hooked when she first visited for a pub lunch in 2006, saying: "If that's what a pub lunch is, I look forward to the next one." So when the Queen is staying in Lancashire's Ribble Valley – usually in her capacity as Duke (yes Duke) of Lancaster – she knows she can mosey on down to her 'local', just down the road from where she stays with friends.

Her friendship was also extended to the landlord of the Inn at Whitewell, Charles Bowman, the third generation of his family to run the hotel, restaurant and pub. Since Her Majesty indirectly owns the Inn – and the entire Whitewell Estate, through the Duchy of Lancaster – discretion is a given, as is a low-key and unfussy welcome. For the Queen's 80th birthday, the Duke of Edinburgh organised an anniversary lunch at the Inn, which went down well with 'Brenda', as her children and many in the Royal family privately call her... though not to her face.

So what are the Inn's attractions – both for the Queen and the general public? For starters, it's the perfect place to relax and be yourself. At her first pub lunch visit, staff treated the Queen with respect, but felt free to engage. The food's of a high standard, made with 'seriously good local ingredients', and patrons are an interesting mix of locals, walkers, fishing folk and birdwatchers. Little wonder that the Queen told her biographer that the Ribble Valley is on her retirement wish list. Little wonder, too, that this former 14th-century manor house turned coaching inn was named Pub of the Year in 2020. It's also accessible, being just a 45-minute drive from the heart of Lancaster over the Trough of Bowland Pass. As a bonus, part of the route has spectacular views over Morecambe Bay and the Lake District fells.

Address Forest of Bowland, Lancashire, BB7 3AT, +44 (0)120 0448 222, www.innatwhitewell.com | **Getting there** By car, from Lancaster, along Wyresdale Road, up Quernmore Brow over the Trough of Bowland | **Hours** Lunch served noon–2pm | **Tip** Try crossing the stepping stones across the River Hodder just below the Inn's terrace – but do so before lunch or dinner, or you might be the 'wet, wet, wet' spectacle for those looking out!

49 Jenny Brown's Point

A lady, a lost lover and tales of the sea

The sad story of Jenny Brown still hangs over the coastal stretches of salt marsh and rocky outcrops between Silverdale and Carnforth on the northern flank of Morecambe Bay. According to legend, the local lass sat on the rocks every day, looking wistfully out to sea, waiting in vain for her sailor lover to return from war. Many say he was killed in his first battle, months after setting sail to fight in the European wars of the early 19th century. But with no confirmation of his fate, Jenny never lost hope. She never married, and when she died, she left the legacy name of Jenny Brown's Point.

Jenny – Christened Jennet – lived with her parents in Brown's Cottage, which still stands as a Grade II-listed building, just above the shoreline. But by far the most notable structure on the seashore is a stone-built chimney, standing alone, with the sea lapping right up to its base. It has become a celebrated landmark, itself a listed structure. It's stood proud for over 230 years since it was built to draw air through a long-gone copper-smelting furnace. A legal wrangle over the rights to copper mining nearby ended in the project being abandoned in 1788.

Then there's 'Walduck's Wall' – an attempt to reclaim 6,300 acres of land on the north bay shore by Manchester metal merchant Herbert Walduck. After political rows and local outrage, the scheme was trimmed back. Limestone rocks were dumped into the sea to form a mile-long 'pier' to hold back the tides, but the scheme was abandoned in 1879 when the funds ran dry. The shifting sands covered the pier, but in 1975, the stones reappeared, and can be seen to this day.

Added to all this is the dramatic sinking in 1894 of the pleasure yacht *Matchless*, when a sudden squall off Jenny Brown's Point capsized the vessel, resulting in 25 deaths. Safety regulations were tightened, but too late to help those aboard *Matchless*.

Address LA5 0UA | **Getting there** By car, five minutes from Silverdale Village; walk takes 30 minutes along Lindeth Road; bus 51 from Carnforth Station to Silverdale Village, then a 15-minute walk, or train from Carnforth to Silverdale Station, then bus 51 to the village | **Hours** Always accessible | **Tip** Circular walk of a little over five miles from Silverdale National Trust car park just beyond Silverdale Station; breath-taking views, paths and coves en route to Jenny Brown's Point (arnsidesilverdaleaonb.org.uk).

50__ The Jigsaw Lounge
Putting the pieces together in Kirkby Lonsdale

If you're keen to puzzle over putting a few pieces in a jigsaw, pop into The Jigsaw Lounge in Kirkby Lonsdale, known locally as 'KL' (see ch. 55). There's always one on the go inside the shop, which is dedicated to the jigsaw – a long-established form of wholesome entertainment that the whole family can enjoy. Following the success of a venture called the Market Jigsaw Exchange, open for business every Thursday at the town's once-a-week Charter Market, it was decided to open an outlet dedicated to 'the satisfying art' in nearby Main Street – number 18, to be precise, just a few doors away from its well-established sister shop, The Book Lounge, at number 12.

The cerebral act of composing jigsaws is taken very seriously, with stocks of Ravensburger, Gibsons, House of Puzzles, and Falcon jigsaws among those on sale, alongside the swap shop activity – subject to a small exchange fee – and the sale of boards and sorting trays. It's a serious, but joyful, business.

It's all part of the vision of owner Valerie Laycock, who was school librarian at Central Lancaster High School for more than 17 years. Her love of books and jigsaws resulted in her double initiative. After the interest generated by her weekly market stall, she decided to open a dedicated jigsaw shop. She opens daily, and encourages people to buy a takeaway coffee and homemade cake from the Book Lounge and take them into the Jigsaw Lounge.

There, you realise that there's more to jigsaws than meets the eye. Valerie's 'special interest' jigsaws include 3D puzzles, with depictions of Big Ben, the Eiffel Tower and a VW camper van. Then there's the 1,000-piece 'Escape Puzzle', where the player is plunged into a 'mystifying world', with instructions in a sealed envelope. There's even a jigsaw where you have to find 15 differences between the image on the box and the finished jigsaw. Some jigsaws have randomly-shaped pieces to add a further challenge.

Address 18 Main Street, Kirkby Lonsdale, LA6 2AG, www.thejigsawlounge.shop | **Getting there** Bus 81 and 582 from Lancaster almost hourly; by car, 16 miles from Lancaster on the B6254, up the Lune Valley, passing M6 J34 | **Hours** Mon–Sat 10am–4.30pm | **Tip** Number 44 Café on Main Street is interesting, with its distinctive, purple-splashed decor; it offers wonderful home-made scones and a wide variety of vegan offerings, with friendly service.

51 John Lawson's Grave

Quaker Meeting House memorial

The grave of John Lawson has a special significance in Lancaster's rich Quaker history. For starters, its large, vernacular style of lettering is very distinctive. Unusually, it also stands upright, and is inside the Friends' Meeting House near Lancaster Railway Station. It honours one of the city's first converts to the Quaker belief – by the movement's founder, George Fox himself.

The gravestone is in the entrance porch to the Meeting House, which was built in the early 18th century. Lawson himself became a 'Friend' back in 1652, when Fox visited Lancaster. The charismatic leader preached in the market square, then caused outrage and uproar when he entered Lancaster Parish Church during a service. When he was chased off by the congregation, Fox sought sanctuary in Lawson's shop in St Leonardsgate, and the owner soon became a Quaker adherent and a follower.

However, with apologies to Clint Eastwood and Sergio Leone, Lawson epitomised *The Good, the Bad and the Ugly*. The 'good' aspect was that he became one of the Quaker's 'Valiant Sixty' – a group of key activists and travelling preachers who helped lift people's spirits in pretty desperate times. The 'bad' aspect was that Lawson owed his wealth to sugar, which was produced by slave labour in the West Indies. The 'ugly' was the way that many of Lancaster's Georgian business fraternity lived their lives of charm and gentility, without seeing or caring for the slave element in the lucrative triangular trade. Manufactured goods went to West Africa; the captured slaves were shipped from there to the Caribbean; and the raw materials produced on the slave plantations – including sugar – were brought over to Lancaster, where actual slaves were rarely seen; out of sight, out of mind. Once a Quaker, Lawson suffered for his beliefs, being imprisoned in Chester, Preston and twice in Lancaster.

Address Friends' Meeting House, Meeting House Lane, Lancaster, LA1 1TX, lancasterquakers@btinternet.com | **Getting there** Next to the railway station; by car, just off the A6 (north) route through Lancaster | **Hours** Meetings for worship Sun 10.30–11.30am, Wed 12.40–1pm; arrange visits with the warden by email | **Tip** Visit the Old Quaker Cemetery on the Moor at Golgotha, 86, Wyresdale Road on the southern edge of Williamson Park; an interesting, overgrown location with a characterful porch entry.

52 John O'Gaunt Castle
Where the Queen is toasted as a Duke!

The grim-looking face above Lancaster Castle's hugely-impressive gateway is hardly noticed by the casual visitor – but it's the reason why our present Queen is called the Duke of Lancaster, despite being a woman! The title has been passed down to the reigning monarch since 1399 after John O'Gaunt – the man with the grim face – became the first Duke of Lancaster.

The Duchy, which owns the beautifully-preserved and well-maintained Lancaster Castle, is a unique collection of land, property and assets held in trust for whomsoever is Sovereign. It's been this way since the 13th century, when Henry III gifted the baronial land to his son Edmund. Further privileges came Lancashire's way when Edward III raised its status to a 'County Palatine', with the Duke of Lancaster enjoying devolved Royal powers. Queen Victoria insisted on keeping the title 'Duke', believing the word 'Duchess' inferred she was the spouse of the title holder. Hence, our Queen today is a duke.

She is said to savour the title, and no doubt the revenue raised on her behalf: the Duchy raises a cool £23 million in annual income for the Queen. The Duchy owns almost 46,000 acres of land holdings, including farmland and rural estates, urban developments, historic buildings such as Lancaster Castle, and commercial properties throughout England and Wales. This includes the revenue-rich Savoy Estate in London's West End, taking in the Savoy Hotel on the Strand.

All the work is done by Duchy staff at its London headquarters, overseen politically by the MP chosen as the Chancellor of the Duchy of Lancaster, a position that occasionally has full Cabinet rank. At all public dinners in the County Palatine, the after-meal toast is always to the Queen and the Duke of Lancaster. When in the Duchy, the Queen often stays in the Ribble Valley, and hinted to her biographer that she would be happy to retire there.

Address Castle Grove, Lancaster, LA1 1YN, www.lancastercastle.com | Getting there
300-metres from Lancaster railway station; by car, signposted from M6 J34 northbound;
if travelling south, exit J33; car parking available at nearby Dallas Road | Hours Daily
9.30am–5pm except the Christmas/New Year period; daily guided tours | Tip A five-
minute walk down Market Street is the John O'Gaunt Horseshoe, set in paving stones at
the intersection of Penny Street and Cheapside. It is said that his horse lost the shoe when
he left Lancaster for the last time.

53 The Judges' Lodgings
Childs' play in Lancaster's hanging house

For a house with strong connections to Lancaster's reputation as 'the hanging town', the old Judges' Lodgings has a few unexpected and quite quirky claims to fame. It was the first home in Lancaster to have window shutters, not only as a safety feature to keep the house secure, but also as a way of insulating against heat loss – quite an advance in its day. Nowadays, the public can go in for a small fee, though children are not charged. This is only appropriate, given the historic building houses a Museum of Childhood, with old-fashioned children's toys to play with, the opportunity to engage in a little craft work, and the chance to play family games or even have a picnic in the garden.

So what's the sinister aspect to the house? What are the elements that send a shiver down the spine? For a start, this stylish home, the oldest townhouse in the city, was built back in 1625 by Keeper of the Castle, Thomas Covell – the man responsible for locking up the Pendle Witches during the infamous Lancashire Witch Trials. By 1826, the premises had become lodgings for the 'Red Judges' of the Assize Courts. Dressed in their scarlet robes, the judges presided over the fate of murderers, highwaymen and forgers, who were sent to Lancaster for trial from all over the county of Lancashire. At that time, the county stretched from the old Westmorland and Cumberland border in the north, to the growing cities of Manchester and Liverpool in the south. Little wonder that Lancaster gained its 'hanging town' notoriety.

Today, the museum houses a large collection of highly-prized Georgian furniture, made by Gillows of Lancaster (see ch. 37), with the hallowed pieces gracing the large number of period rooms. There's an authentic kitchen, complete with open fire and side ovens, and a walled courtyard and garden, which provides a 'green oasis' and picnic area in the heart of the city.

Address Church Street, Lancaster, LA1 1YS, www.lancashire.gov.uk/museums | Getting there Five-minute walk from Lancaster bus station or Lancaster railway station | Hours Spring to early Nov, Fri–Sun 11am–4pm | Tip The house is reputed to be the first home of distinction in Lancaster, and in front of it is a cross on a circular plinth dedicated to its builder, Thomas Covell.

54 Kent Estuary Tidal Bore
Surfing USA... that's 'Up Stream Arnside'

While not exactly Hawaii or San Jose in California, it's quite possible to surf up the Kent Estuary at Arnside when conditions are favourable. Rather than huge waves crashing against the shore, the Arnside experience is a single tidal bore, or wave. Although you might not see hundreds of sun-tanned surf dudes braving the Pacific rollers, you do see wet-suited devotees and kayakers taking the opportunity to ride the tide. Predicting its occurrence is always an issue, but crowds of sightseers line Arnside Pier and promenade to watch the bore crash into Arnside Viaduct when the timings have worked out.

The tidal bore is a rare phenomenon that occurs in only a few locations in the world: the most famous in the UK is the Severn Bore, which reaches quite a height as it funnels into the River Severn from the wide Bristol Channel. In the Kent Estuary, it can reach a couple of feet, rising in height as the water funnels up the restricted channel. It's best seen or experienced in spring when the tides are high, although bores can occur right through until September. This is unsurprising when considering that the waters from the 120-square-mile vastness of Morecambe Bay are concentrated on the channel of the River Kent, which can carry quite a volume of outflowing water itself, being fed by the Lake District mountains and fells.

Conditions are most propitious when there is a particularly high tide, a low pressure zone over the Irish Sea, a strong onshore wind driving the tidal waters from the west, and a large volume of run-off water in the Kent. Typically, a bore occurs about two hours before high tide. Helpfully, a siren is sounded twice before each daylight tide by Arnside Coastguards. The first time is 15 to 20 minutes before a potential bore is due, the second siren being sounded as the waters reach Blackstone Point just down the Kent Estuary.

Address Anywhere from Arnside's Promenade to Blackstone Point | Getting there From the Albion pub near the roundabout on Arnside Promenade, find a vantage point | Hours Check with locals for tidal bore expectations from March to September | Tip Have a coffee, a cake, or an ice cream at Arnside Beach Hut, just behind Arnside Coastguard Station on the Promenade pathway (+44 (0)7488 227617).

55 Kirkby Lonsdale View

Turner landscape inspires the great 'JR' in 'KL'

The old Westmorland market town of Kirkby Lonsdale is charming enough in its own right – an ancient community with no shortage of characterful and quaint buildings, and a host of independent traders. But 'KL', as it's known locally, is also doubly blessed with artistic connections, particularly the luminary figures of J. M. W. Turner and John Ruskin.

The latter knew of Turner's acclaimed watercolour of the panoramic view from high up above the River Lune, a painting he composed from a sketch made back in 1816. Being a devotee of Turner, Ruskin was determined to visit the vantage point, which is just beyond the churchyard of St Mary the Virgin's. When he did so in 1875, he was astonished by its majesty and beauty. In his finest lyrical manner, he wrote: 'I do not know in all my country, still less in France and Italy, a place more naturally divine.' From that time onwards, what was 'Turner's View' became known as 'Ruskin's View'.

The celebrated art critic and social observer set the scene for KL, which still attracts visitors to look out over the upper reaches of the Lune – a very different river from that which runs through Lancaster 17 miles downstream. In the distance are the Underley Hills, the Middleton Fells and, in the south east, the top of Ingleborough in North Yorkshire. From the promenade viewing point is a stone pulpit with a map that explains the various hills and fells on the horizon.

In 2012, Turner's watercolour known as *Ruskin's View* came up for auction at Bonhams in London, fetching over £215,000 – the first time it had been seen in public since 1884. 'KL' itself is an interesting place to visit, especially on market day, which is every Thursday. The town has had a market since 1227, and still offers a vibrant and bustling array of stalls, pubs, cafés and interesting shops, such as the puzzling Jigsaw Lounge (see ch. 50).

Address Kirkby Lonsdale, Carnforth, LA6 2BB | **Getting there** By car, from M 6 J 34, take the A 683 to Kirby Lonsdale | **Hours** Always accessible | **Tip** In the corner of the churchyard is an unusual, stone-built, hexagonal folly, known as 'The Gazebo'; it has a castle-like roof feature, and outside steps.

56 Lancaster Brewery
Cheers to local brews made good

Lancaster Brewery is a highly successful business – but started out as the wistful dream of two students at Lancaster University to run a bar. Many years on, Phil Simpson and Matt Jackson bought the Water Witch pub in Lancaster's 'Canal Quarter', and later the run-down Sun Inn, based in a Georgian building in Church Street. They began brewing beer in an old Lancaster assembly unit, which used to make cockpits for Hurricane fighter aircraft.

Today, their modern Lancaster Brewery premises in Lancaster Leisure Park is a major producer, and a popular visitor attraction too. It has its own Brewhouse and Tap bar for visitors, as well as conducted tours, with a huge range of types, tastes and strengths on offer. There's a core range of Lancaster Blonde, Amber, Red and Black, though the range has also included such offerings as Lancaster Rum and Raisin and Lancaster Raspberry Rose! More than 40,000 pints a week are produced. The brewery sells more than a million bottles a year to supermarkets and around 400 pubs. It's now as much a part of Lancaster's furniture as the Gillows were in their heyday (see ch. 38).

Locals and visitors alike can visit the Brewhouse Tap bar, where they can savour the products and mix and mingle. There are three official tours of the brewery, all lasting 45 minutes, to see the full brewing process from milling right through to fermentation and maturation. The Amber Tour includes five samples at the bar after the walk-round; the Blonde Tour includes a Brewer's snack of typical Lancashire fare of homemade pork pie and pickles or a pizza, with up to three pints. Then there's the Red Tour with pie and peas and up to four pints. Of course, the brewery is open for special bookings, with stag or hen nights, actual receptions, and visits by organisations and societies. Education, interest and pleasure all in one package.

Address Lancaster Brewery, Lancaster Leisure Park, Wyresdale Road, Lancaster, LA1 3LA, www.lancasterbrewery.co.uk | Getting there A 35-minute walk from Lancaster bus station via Moor Lane and Wyresdale Road; bus 18 is infrequent but direct and takes around 20 minutes, or several buses towards the university, then a mile walk from the Bowerham Hotel | Hours Sun noon – 7pm, Wed & Thu noon – 8pm, Fri & Sat noon – 10pm | Tip For a real ale boozer with a classic Lancaster connection, try Ye Olde John O' Gaunt in Market Street in the city centre: characterful, with a wide selection of ales, and loud live music at weekends.

57__Lancaster Grand

Haunting history of theatre's 'Grey Lady'

It seems to be a statutory requirement for any established theatre to have at least one resident ghost – and it's a near certainty when you're talking about a venue that's been around for almost 250 years. Lancaster's Grand Theatre dates back to 1782, when it first opened its doors, which makes it the third-oldest theatre in Britain. Its opening took place back in the day when George III was still on the throne, and when, to give historical context, the United States of America was gaining its independence.

Just 13 years after the theatre's opening, actress Sarah Siddons played Lady Macbeth, wife of Shakespeare's tragic hero. Years later, when Sarah died, her spirit is said to have lived on, and to this day staff and visitors at The Grand swear that an apparition – known as 'The Grey Lady' – can be seen drifting across the auditorium or sitting in the stalls. Paranormal investigators also claim that the spirit of a travelling actor called 'Harald' can be detected in the same vicinity. Little is known about the mysterious Harald, except that he stayed at Morecambe's Art Deco Midland Hotel in 1937. Many witnesses claim to feel a chill in the air at the very moment the ghostly apparitions appear in front of them.

Regardless of such happenings, The Grand is an imposing spectacle in its own right. Today's 460-seat, two-tier theatre is an Edwardian masterpiece, having been rebuilt in 1908 following a major fire. Its sumptuous gold and red decor is impressive. The theatre hosts both amateur and professional shows, and is run by the registered charity 'Lancaster Footlights', which saved the theatre from demolition in 1951. They have well-advanced plans for a new reception, foyer and bar space to give an exciting entrance and facilities, as well as another extension for a rehearsal space, workshop, costume department and a scenery storage facility. The Grand hosts both amateur and professional shows, plays and events.

Address St Leonard's Gate, Lancaster, LA1 1NL, +44 (0)1524 64695, www.lancastergrand.co.uk | Getting there Four-minute walk from Lancaster bus station | Hours Booking office 10am–3pm | Tip Guided tours of the theatre are available, with the opportunity to stand on the stage in the auditorium, which has a circular balcony and ornate plasterwork, as well as venturing backstage. You might even see a ghost!

58 Lancaster Smokehouse
Haaf way nets success

Michael Price not only runs the Port of Lancaster Smokehouse, he also catches much of the produce himself – and does so in the old-fashioned way. In traditional fisherman's oilskins, Michael stands up to his chest in the tidal River Lune, using the old, hand-held 'haaf net' – a fishing implement and technique brought over by the Vikings a thousand years ago.

Twice a day, Michael can be out in the river, bracing himself against the ebb or flood tidal flow, holding up the five-metre net, which is supported by three wooden poles. Holding the central pole, he tilts it backwards when he feels a fish hit the net, then scoops the net upwards to secure the fish. For conservation reasons, catching salmon is outlawed at present, but he is able to catch sea trout and other species, including whitebait and shrimp. All of Michael's catch goes to his family-run smokehouse and fish business near Glasson Dock, on the south side of the Lune. The company supplies smoked fish, meats and cheeses to restaurants, shops and customers who call in to the smokehouse shop at the side of a small industrial estate near Glasson Dock itself. Traditional methods of smoking and curing are used, 'with nothing added, apart from salt, smoke and time'.

To Michael, now in his 40s, fishing is a way of life, having been in the business for more than 25 years. He is, however, one of a dwindling number of haaf netters on the Lune, with only a dozen holding a licence. His father John started the smokehouse in a small building on St George's Quay in Lancaster around 50 years ago. It was little more than a hobby at first, but as orders from restaurants increased, Michael joined the company to help out. At their Port of Lancaster premises, as well as local produce, mackerel and herring are brought in from Peterhead in Scotland, while Arbroath Smokies are brought from the town after which they are named.

Address Glasson Dock, LA2 0DB, +44 (0)1524 751493, www.lancastersmokehouse.co.uk | **Getting there** Buses are infrequent from Lancaster to Glasson Dock; by car, from Lancaster, taking Aldcliffe Road to Ashton Road/A 588, then B 5290; walking or cycling follows the Lune Estuary Footpath | **Hours** Mon – Fri 9am – 5pm, Sat & Sun 10am – 4pm | **Tip** There are several cafés in Glasson Dock, including Lantern O'er Lune, Lockkeepers Restaurant, and The Shop.

59 Levens Hall Topiary

Join the chess set and cut a dash

It's a real Narnia experience, but the entrance to the magical world is not through a wardrobe, as in the work of author C. S. Lewis, but is in this instance a small, hole-in-the-wall gateway. This leads suddenly into the wondrous and magical gardens of Levens Hall, a short distance over the Cumbrian border, but just 20 miles north of Lancaster. There, hidden behind a high stone wall, lie 10 acres of impressive gardens, including what is claimed to be the oldest topiary garden in the world. Ancient box trees and yews abound, and in keeping with the surreal entrance experience, there are the huge abstract and geometrically-shaped topiary displays that are unique to Levens.

The amazing topiary garden is certainly a cut above the rest. More than 100 specimens have been cut into shapes ranging from monstrous chess pieces to pyramids and a variety of large abstract displays. Some of the trees and hedges are more than 300 years old. They were first created by the French gardener Guillaume Beaumont, who laid out the gardens in 1694, followed by the nearby deer park, with the results surviving largely intact.

Levens Hall itself is a magnificent Elizabethan mansion built around a 13th-century defensive pele tower, which was expanded and rebuilt towards the end of the 16th century. The house is the home of the Bagots, whose family have been in continuous ownership for more than 400 years. It contains an impressive collection of Jacobean furniture, fine paintings, and many other beautiful objects. However, no doubt Guillaume would say it is the garden that is the *piece de resistance*.

The hall also has a small collection of steam road vehicles, including a number of traction engines, which are usually steamed up on Sundays and Bank Holidays. It is an intriguing place to visit for all the family. The Levens Kitchen café is an added attraction.

Address Levens Hall, LA8 0PD | **Getting there** By car, from M6, leave at Junction 35 and join the A6 north; the hall is on the left, two miles or so past Milnthorpe | **Hours** 28 Mar to 7 Oct | **Tip** Look out for St George's Tower, on a hill overlooking the A6 on the left as you come back into Milnthorpe from Levens Hall; a summerhouse folly built to commemorate the 1832 Reform Act; visually attractive but with no public access.

60 Little Sambo's Grave

Tragedy of a slave child

Just a short walk from Sunderland Point's old quay is the unconsecrated grave of child slave, Little Sambo. Nowadays, the name could come straight from the politically-incorrect lexicon, but the story of his grave, its upkeep and its symbolism is heartening to all. It also acts as a modern-day reminder of Lancaster's part in the terrible slave trade of the 18th and 19th centuries.

Sambo was a 14-year-old boy from West Africa who became a servant to a ship's master. He had done two legs of the notorious triangular trade route, having been captured in West Africa, taken to the West Indies, then brought back to the ship's home port on the River Lune in 1736. Neither the name of the ship nor that of her master are known, but the master left Sambo at Sunderland Point's brew house on the quay while he went on to Lancaster on business. Either Sambo felt deserted or he contracted a European disease on landing. Whatever the cause, he went into a stupefied state, laid out on the bare boards of the attic, and refused all offers of food and drink. He died just a few days later.

However, the heartening aspect of this sad story is that the sailors on the ship felt he should be buried, although they had to do this in an unconsecrated plot near the sea shore, away from the village. A plaque was put on the grave, reading: *Here lies Poor Sambo, a faithful negro.* Years on, in 1796, a schoolmaster in Lancaster heard the story and wrote a poem which read: 'Then the Grateful Judge his Approbation found, Not on man's colour but his worth of heart.'

Today, flowers and coloured stones are left by local children, and in 2019, the grave was enclosed by a low stone wall. The original brass plaque, put on the grave by well-wishers, was stolen, but subsequently replaced. In the end, 'Poor Sambo' was afforded respect and peaceful repose.

Address LA3 3HP | **Getting there** By car, from Lancaster, head for A 589/Bay Gateway/A 683, turn left to Overton, then across the tidal road to Sunderland Point; five-minute walk to the grave | **Hours** Daylight hours at low tide only – check tide times | **Tip** Sunderland Point Old Hall at the far end of the village has a West Indian-style balcony, which represents clear evidence of the Atlantic trade. The rounded, overhead canopy gave shelter from the sun in the Caribbean – but probably the rain in Sunderland Point!

61 Longhouse of Heysham

Lancashire's longhouse tradition lives on

There aren't many 17th-century village longhouses that have survived in the old county of Lancashire, so it's highly appropriate that a rare historical example should be the home of the Heysham Heritage Association. The original longhouse comprised a domestic cottage and a barn in one long, linear building. It was traditionally a place where an extended family would live, often alongside their animals and provisions. Heysham's longhouse is situated in the village's Main Street, and as such is the perfect place to show the inquisitive visitor what changes have happened over time.

So far, more than 100,000 visitors have come through the door to see the features of the ancient longhouse barn, where the Heritage Association displays are housed. Visitors can look at old photographs, historical artefacts, talk to local historians and examine Heysham's official history timeline. This stretches back to the village's early Viking settlement days of the 10th century, taking the visitor right up to Heysham's nuclear power stations of the present day. The exhibit puts a wider context on any date selected. For example, Heysham's famous rock-cut graves of the eighth century are matched with 750 AD, telling when Offa came to the throne of Mercia. Another highlighted date is 937 AD, when Norse, Scottish and Irish invaders combined in a bid to unseat King Athelstan, the last major battle before William the Conqueror arrived on English soil to change the course of history yet again. Little wonder that one visitor felt that the Heysham 'longhouse' was 'a little piece of Heaven'.

The next door cottage garden has been restored by volunteers, though it can only be visited during summer open days. The village itself has 26 listed buildings, with the longhouse dating back to the days when Heysham was a quiet farming and fishing community, before Heysham Port opened in 1904.

Address Main Street, Heysham Village, LA3 2RW, www.heyshamheritage.org.uk | Getting there By car, from M6 J34, follow road signs for Heysham, then brown signs for Heysham Village | Hours See website for summer opening times (Apr–Sep) and winter opening (Oct only) | Tip More difficult to find nowadays, but nettle beer was an absolute must for visitors to Heysham Village. Traditionally made by local resident Granny Hutchinson, the non-alcoholic tonic was made from herbal extracts, yeast, lemons, sugar, and, of course, nettles.

62 Lovers' Knott Tree

Larch Ascending, high above the Kent Estuary

It's a totally unexpected sight, and a real talking point for walkers, and for locals, who are proud of having a quirky and welcoming feature at the top of Arnside Knott. The focal point of any walk up the Knott – meaning 'hill' – is a knotted larch tree. In fact, it's two larch trees 'knotted' together, some say by two lovers. As they grew together, so did the two trees. Because of its shape, some call it 'the H tree', while others call it 'the giraffe tree'. It's all a matter of preference. The weathered feature has been there for decades, with more naturally-weathered larch stumps to be found near the hillside walks that criss-cross the hill. The Knott itself is a nature lover's delight, and that's on top of the majestic views of the Kent Estuary and Morecambe Bay, with Grange-over-Sands and the Lake District fells above the far shore.

On the Knott itself, take a walk to the trig point at the very top of the hill and you might see some Lancashire whitebeams. Blending into their environment, they're not striking in any photographer's eyes, but they are said to exist only here in the limestone soils around Morecambe Bay. Continue your walk along the slopes of the Knott and you'll see wind-shaped juniper trees hugging the rocky screes. Spreading low across the ground like green shrubs, these conifers are hundreds of years old, but have been grazed by passing deer and sculpted into all sorts of shapes and sizes. Constant nibbling by deer and rabbits means that they don't reproduce very easily, making them a priority species for conservation.

There are also mature yew trees, many of which are more than 400 years old. Old lime trees are quite profuse: when they drop a bough, it can root again and gradually colonise the area. Another quirky feature of this Area of Outstanding Natural Beauty are the hand-made wooden gates, usually made of ash. Local volunteers use traditional techniques to split, cut and join the wood.

Address Arnside Knott car park, LA5 0BP | Getting there From Arnside, take Silverdale Road, turn right into Red Hills Road and continue for 0.6 miles; keep left on to Knott Lane and Saul's Drive; take the track to the car park | Hours Daytime year-round | Tip Stock up with a picnic of pies and sandwiches from The Old Bakehouse, in the row opposite Arnside Pier, and when you return, you can have traditional fish and chips from Arnside Chipshop near the viaduct.

63 Lune Estuary Marshes

Nurturing nature, far from the muddying crowd

The old song goes: 'Mud, mud, glorious mud, nothing quite like it for cooling the blood'. It may be about a hippo rolling in the sticky stuff, but as you stare out on the vast expanses of salt marsh and mud channels in the Lune Estuary and on the nearby coast, the refrain comes to mind immediately. The tide-washed area can be bleak but also beautiful in its own right, particularly the colours of the increasingly-rare, purple-blue sea lavender, which comes alive on parts of Lancashire's salt marshes in summer.

Of equal importance is the fact that the marshes and glistening mud channels are a bountiful supplier of food for wildlife, particularly our feathered friends. The area supports large populations of winter waders and water fowl, as well as an amazing array of all-year or seasonal visitors. It is a nursery for nature areas like the Lune Estuary and the coastal strips both north of the river mouth, and south on the Cockerham, and then Wyre coasts. The details of this feeding and breeding ground might not sound too alluring – a home for bristle worms, mud snails and bi-valves – but it attracts an abundance of bird life from as far away as the Arctic climes, and as far east as Siberia.

In north Lancashire, at RSPB Leighton Moss reed beds, the Bittern from the Russian Urals has returned to breed, along with the Avocet, which was thought to have vanished from Britain decades ago. The waders and migration species are drawn to the sea marshes, as are the lapwing and curlews from the Lancashire moors, the peregrine falcon, mergansers, redshank, oyster catchers and the skylark. There's a well-conducted orchestra of avian sounds. The salt marshes are also a seedbed for luscious green sanfire, swaying cord grasses, sea parslane and those beautiful summer sea lavenders. So long as the beds are covered and washed regularly by sea water, the system works.

Address A useful starting point is the Stork Hotel at Conder Green, LA2 0AN | Getting there Regular bus service from Lancaster to Glasson Dock and Cockerham; on foot, walk along the Lancashire Coastal Path from Lancaster | Hours Visit during daylight for safety | Tip Less than a mile from the nearby Port of Lancaster is Hebbs Alpacas, where you can meet and greet the alpacas, or even lead one on a walk. This family-run farm is located off Jeremy Lane, near Glasson Dock.

64 Lyth Valley
Fruitfulness of the Damson Scene

Roadside stalls selling newly-harvested autumnal fruit is a pretty routine sight in many rural areas – and this is the case in the Lyth Valley. But there's one big difference in this sheltered valley: surrounded by protective limestone hills, and with its own special micro-climate. In the Lyth Valley grows the distinctive Westmorland Damson – and that's what can be found on country lane stalls during harvest time in mid to late September.

Traditionally, each small farmstead is surrounded by a damson orchard, and most hedgerows in the Lyth Valley include damson trees too. This makes for a spectacle of continuous snow-white blossom in April or early May, depending on weather conditions. Such is the spring-time attraction, that in the inter-war years, hundreds of charabancs would bring visitors from all over Lancashire to see the magnificent sight.

Come early autumn, the emphasis turns to food and drink, as the versatile Westmorland Damson tickles the taste buds. Offerings include chutney, jam, puddings, and a local favourite, damson gin. Although the Westmorland Damson is a member of the plum family, the unique conditions of the Lyth Valley mark it out as something special. It's claimed that the added 'secret ingredient' is pollination by two of the damson's cousins – the bullace and the sloe, both being thorny, berry-bearing bushes or small trees that grow wild in the area.

How the damson came to grow here is open to speculation, with theories that the fruit was brought back from Damascus by Crusading knights, or by Roman legions on their way to Hadrian's Wall. The fruit's importance led to the formation of the Westmorland Damson Association, which holds a celebratory Damson Day, highlighting the April blossom and the September harvest. Cowmire Hall, LA8 8JJ, near Crossthwaite in the Lyth Valley, has taken over hosting April's Damson Day activities.

Address Cowmire Hall, Kendal, LA8 8JJ, www.lythdamsons.org.uk | Getting there By car, on the A6 north, follow Barrow signs on the A590, turn right at Beck End, LA11 6RH, then follow towards Crossthwaite village | Hours Year-round on public roads, with Damson Day in April | Tip Foulshaw Moss Nature Reserve, off the A590, has a pair of breeding ospreys every year; a live webcam streams them between spring and autumn, when the birds and their offspring return to West Africa (www.cumbriawildlifetrust.org).

65 Market Cross Memorial

Crowning glory of a memorable bus shelter

It's probably the most ornate bus shelter ever constructed. Not that Kirkby Lonsdale's Market Cross Memorial set out to protect waiting bus passengers from any manner of climatic conditions. Nevertheless, the covered memorial is most welcome to passers-by, passengers, and those attending the town's famous Charter Market, which dates back to the 13th century. The memorial was built in loving memory of the wife of Kirkby Lonsdale vicar, the Rev. J. W. Davies, who presented it to the town in 1905. The octagonal stone structure was built in the Tudor-Gothic style and has Grade II-listed status.

It's an impressive structure, and was even more embellished during its first four decades of existence. In the centre, a series of arched stone pieces reached for the heavens and met in the middle. It was twice as high as the present structure. However, with fears of passing traffic loosening the heavy stone pieces on top, potentially leading to dangerous collapse, they were removed in the late 1940s, leaving a structure that looks like a crown to this day. Officially, it has 'an octagonal stone canopy, with pyramidal slate roof.' Inside are seats, which are most welcome for shoppers laden with market day produce and waiting for buses home to surrounding villages. Every Thursday, scores of stalls set up in the old Georgian square, now known as Market Square. The initial 13th-century market was held at the other end of Main Street, where it links up with Market Street. However, the market's expansion resulted in the move to its current location.

Initially, the town had separate markets for pigs, horses and cattle, the latter being linked to Main Street by Salt Pie Lane, so named after an enterprising lady, who sold well-salted mutton pies to market traders. When her customers were desperate for a drink, they went to the nearby Green Dragon pub – now the Snooty Fox – which was owned, conveniently, by a relative of hers.

Address Market Square, Kirkby Lonsdale, LA6 2AN | Getting there By car, just off the A 65 by the Royal Hotel; parking available in nearby New Road; bus 582 runs hourly from Lancaster bus station throughout the day | Hours Always accessible; markets Thu 9am–4pm | Tip The Enchanted Chocolate Mine is a small but fun attraction in the cellar of the shop, Chocolat on New Road, opposite Market Square. Aimed at 'the young and young at heart', it shows how the faeries work the chocolate mines. For those able to negotiate the steep stone cellar steps, it's quite delightful, and free (www.chocolatinkl.co.uk).

66 Marlborough Road

Anthony Newley's route to fame

Actor, singer and film star Anthony Newley owes a lot to little More-cambe. As a poor Cockney child, he was evacuated from the East End of London to the North West resort during the Second World War, and the couple who looked after him not only gave him love and security, they also introduced him to the world of theatre, entertainment and the arts.

It was nine-year-old Anthony's luck to be billeted with George Cornille Pescud, a former music hall entertainer and now an actor-manager. George and his wife Belle lived in a respectable, stone-terraced house in Marlborough Road, just over the Heysham 'border' near Morecambe's West End. The house was close to the Alhambra Theatre, where major productions were put on in the booming resort of the late 1930s and even during wartime. It whetted the appetite of young Anthony, who was encouraged to take an interest in the stage, music, painting and dancing. This was in contrast to the precarious life he led as an illegitimate child being brought up by his mother in the tough conditions of Hackney.

When Anthony returned to London after the war, he applied to the top-notch Italia Conti Academy for budding actors. He impressed them hugely, but couldn't afford the fees. The kindly regime took him on as a tea boy, with the meagre wages ostensibly paying his fees. A few years on, aged 16, he obtained his first film part in *The Adventures of Dusty Bates*, then in 1948 played the Artful Dodger in David Lean's *Oliver*. A seven-year contract with the Rank Organisation followed, and over the next 30 years he starred in films, musicals and as a singer. He reached the Top 40 chart a dozen times, including two number-1 hits. He wrote the lyrics for the 1964 Bond film, *Goldfinger*, and he received an Academy nomination for his joint film score for the Willy Wonka musical. All kick-started in Morecambe by George and Belle Pescud.

Address Marlborough Street, Heysham, LA3 1TL | **Getting there** Three-minute drive or a 10-minute walk from Morecambe station | **Hours** Always accessible | **Tip** Still on the creative front, just down the road in Morecambe's West End, the small commercial Edgelands Gallery can be found on Yorkshire Street. This small, independently-owned gallery, dealing with artworks and prints, provides fine art services throughout the North West. Its name reflects the tidal edge lands of Morecambe Bay.

67 Morecambe Bay Shrimpers

Nobbies style and whammel wonders

Nobody quite knows why the traditional fishing boats of Morecambe Bay are called 'nobbies' and 'whammels'. What is known is that generations of shrimpers and salmon netters have used the vessels, whose designs were developed and perfected over 150 years, starting in the 18th century, but getting the wind in their sales in earnest during the 19th and early 20th centuries. The nobby was made by the Crossthwaite family of Arnside, while the whammel was made by the Woodhouses at Overton, on the north bank of the River Lune, upstream from Sunderland Point.

An example of the traditional whammel can be seen in Lancaster's Maritime Museum, which is housed in the city's 18th-century Customs House on the banks of the Lune on St George's Quay. The vessel, described as 'a pretty day boat', was built with a shallow draft for traditional inshore fishing on the Lune, using drift netting to catch salmon from April to August, though this is outside the law at present, due to low stocks. In winter, the whammel would be used for shrimp trawling in the Bay. Nobbies were designed as fast, gaff-rigged sail boats for use in shallow waters, able to pull a trawling net, then return to port quickly with the perishable catch. Prawners were a common sight off Morecambe, Southport and Fleetwood, and with the expansion of the railway, much of the produce was whisked off for sale to the inland industrial areas of Lancashire and Yorkshire.

With help from the Heritage Lottery Fund, Arnside Sailing Club bought a nobby, called *Severn*, which was built in 1912 by the Crossthwaites: their boat building premises can still be seen, next to the Coastguards on the Promenade walkway just down the estuary from the town. The *Severn* is being restored at David Moss's boatyard at Skippool, near Blackpool, but in years to come she should be returning to her original 'home' in Arnside.

Address Customs House, St George's Quay, Lancaster, LA1 1RB | **Getting there** 15-minute walk from Lancaster railway station or 6-minute walk from Lancaster bus station; by car, M6 J34, then Caton Road and the one-way A6 to Damside Street | **Hours** Daily 10am–4pm, or noon–4pm in winter | **Tip** Walk along St George's Quay to take in the Georgian, five-storey warehouses serving Lancaster when it was England's fourth-biggest port.

68 Murals of Morecambe
Gable end art adds a splash of colour

It's impossible to miss the giant mural called *Big Skies and Shifting Tides*. The latest of Morecambe's huge public artworks can be seen on the gable end of a seafront terrace of houses on Sandylands Promenade, just over the Heysham 'border' from Morecambe proper. Overall, there are in excess of 20 murals completed, with the aim of cheering up local residents and visitors alike, and giving a visual lift to under-utilised areas.

The initial burst of creativity began in the 1990s, with what is called the Poulton Village Mural Trail. Two accomplished local artists – Patricia Hartley and Graham Lowe – created the large-scale images that reflect the history and activities in the Poulton community, which has now been incorporated into Morecambe. Seven murals were created, using render for durability. Many have a nautical theme and Art Deco style, and have the backing of Morecambe Art Colony – a body dedicated to using art for the town's regeneration.

A mural of a fisherman in Wellington boots and oilskins can be found in Fisherman's Square, complete with a three-fish mosaic. Nearby is a depiction of the Clock Tower on Morecambe Promenade, while other artworks can be found in the surrounding streets: a silhouetted fishing boat at sunset; a steam train; the lighthouse on Morecambe's Stone Jetty; a woman cockle-picker out on the sands. All are stunning in their distinctive style, and have been well received.

Another dozen fascinating murals and artworks have been produced by the Morecambe-based creative practice Deco Publique. Several surround the old seafront lido area, with others reflecting the town's sporting connections, birdlife, and mosaic-style depictions of celebrities important to the area, such as Eric Morecambe, Sir Laurence Olivier and Morecambe-born Thora Hird. The 180 square-metre Sandylands mural was also recently completed.

Address 69 Sandylands Promenade, Heysham, LA3 1D | Getting there 25-minute walk or 5-minute drive from Morecambe station | Hours Always accessible | Tip Go for a stroll or run on Sandylands Promenade, either back towards Morecambe, or on towards Heysham, enjoying fabulous views of Morecambe Bay while you exercise.

69 Nuclear Plants

'Energy Central' powers up at the double

Heysham's two nuclear power stations are imposing edifices. The massive, power-packed cubes dominate the skyline, adjacent to the port that serves Ireland and the Isle of Man. Yet there's a huge irony: immediately around the plants and the port are pretty, characterful and historic areas, including the quaint and old-fashioned charm of Heysham Village, with its 17th- and 18th-century cottages. Half a dozen miles up the coast is the traditional resort of Morecambe, soon to be the home of an environmental citadel in the shape of Eden Project North. Just seven miles inland is ancient Lancaster, with its large university population.

For all this, Heysham's two separate power stations have never attracted the same opposition or political 'heat' as nuclear cousin Sellafield, up the coast in Cumbria. Maybe, 30 years or so on, the fear of Armageddon was not as great, and maybe the benefits had become more apparent. Certainly, the message that owners EDF Energy pump out in the Heysham Nuclear Plant Visitor Centre is the mantra of 'secure, clean and affordable energy'.

After taking in the inter-active exhibition centre, visitors are taken into Heysham 2's turbine hall to see the site's reactors and control room. By 2020, Heysham 2 alone generated low-carbon electricity for 2.4 million homes. That's the equivalent of taking 1.4 million cars off the road, and avoids 3.1 million tonnes of CO_2 emissions. The site employs around 750 people, and a recent £24 million maintenance shutdown brought in 1,000 extra contractors. Heysham 1 is operational until 2024, Heysham 2 until at least 2028. Some distance offshore are the Morecambe Bay gas field and wind turbines, and there's constant talk of a bay barrage being built. Heysham is bidding to build the world's first prototype fusion energy plant, generating electricity as a low carbon energy source. With renewables replacing fossil fuels, the world is changing.

Address LA3 2XH | **Getting there** From Heysham Village, follow the A 589 and the A 683 | **Hours** Visitor Centre open Mon–Thu 10am–4pm, Fri 10am–2.30pm, Sat pre-booked tours only | **Tip** For cosy accommodation and good food, try The Royal, a 16th-century inn located in Main Street, Heysham Village (www.theroyalheysham.co.uk).

70__Old Poulton

Doorway to the New World

At first sight, the Gothic-style, arched doorway standing in the middle of a public park is quite mystifying. Even more intriguing is the fact that it was once the entrance to a property owned by ancestors of America's first President, George Washington. The doorway's pointed arch is a structure of obvious antiquity, whereas the surrounding stonework is a modern addition. It's intriguing, and a source of local pride. But why is it there, seemingly marooned and out of place?

The archway is the only remaining element of what was Poulton Hall – and thereby lies a tale. As Poulton's original Manor House, it was given to the monks of Lancaster Priory in 1272. However, the Dissolution of the Monasteries in the 1530s saw the manor divided up between two families, one of which was the Washington family of Warton, near Carnforth. They were the paternal ancestors of George, and it was their family crest – complete with stars and stripes – that influenced the design of the national flag for the newly-independent United States of America (see ch. 35).

The hall was passed down through marriage to various families, eventually becoming a rectory for the nearby parish church. When Poulton became part of Morecambe, it was sold to the Corporation. Eventually, the building was demolished in 1932, the archway being saved and put behind Morecambe Town Hall. It was returned to the original site in 1997, and remains an enigmatic feature to this day: an unlikely link to the New World from an 'old boy' of Lancashire.

A focal point of Old Poulton is Fisherman's Square, whose name reflects the fact that this was once at the heart of the town's fishing activities. A series of colourful outdoor public murals also reflect the fishing heritage. The area was also an important potato-producing area. Perhaps the two activities combined to give us the sea-side fish and chips tradition?

Address 17 Poulton Road, Morecambe, LA4 5HB | **Getting there** 10-minute walk from Morecambe station; buses from the station are frequent | **Hours** Access 24 hours | **Tip** A short walk away on Poulton Road is the 17th-century pub, The Smugglers Den said to be the oldest in Morecambe. It's traditional; it's haunted, of course; and it's said to have had a secret tunnel to the coast.

71 Pennine Tower

Control tower services the M6

The sight of a huge hexagonal Air Traffic Control-style tower at a motorway service station was designed to spark interest, and to be a major talking point for travellers. No one can deny that the 65-foot high 'Pennine Tower' on the M6 at Forton Service Station, seven miles south of Lancaster, succeeded in attracting attention and comment. Built in 1965, the upmarket restaurant and sun deck reflected the ambition of the Concord era, and the in-with-the-new popular culture of the time. It seemed fitting that the Beatles were among its first visitors.

However, the tower never raised a profit for the Rank Organisation, which built the landmark tower as a showpiece for its chain of service stations. A limit of 120 people was placed on the tower, but often the numbers of diners dropped into single figures. Travellers had neither the appetite for fine-dining, nor the time to spend an hour or so eating and looking out over the Morecambe Bay coastline or the Trough of Bowland fells. So, in 1989, new owner Moto, which still runs the services, closed the tower to the public.

Social change and the advent of fast food, and the quick turna-round of customers, killed off the bold venture, and the refusal to allow advertising was a blow. In 2012, it was given Grade II-listed Building status, with National Heritage saying: 'It is time to recognise and appreciate the positive contribution motorways have made to England's heritage.' Three years later, Moto admitted that 'the building has no viable use'. Despite this, it remains a landmark, and Moto claims it to be the most talked-about service station in the country. The tower's two purpose-built lifts, unable to be seen by the public, are of interest to elevator aficionados. They are pentagon shaped to allow them to fit into half of the tower structure, the remaining half accommodating an emergency spiral staircase. Ironically, though it lasted only 24 years, it was designed to take another storey.

Address LA2 9DU | Getting there By car, M6 northbound, between J32 and J33 | Hours Always visible | Tip The M6 Giraffe is a quirky, eye-catching advertising figure by the northbound carriageway between Preston and Lancaster.

72 Penny's Almshouses

William Penny for your thoughts

A small, hole-in-the-wall gateway through a screen wall on the busy A6 in Lancaster leads into an oasis of calm and shelter. Once through the tall, protective perimeter, a charming scene of tranquillity unfolds. A rectangular, cobbled courtyard surrounds an elliptical garden, bedecked in flowers from spring to autumn. A small church stands at the head of the cobbled area. But the main *raison d'etre* for the whole enterprise is the two rows of small cottage homes on either side. The 12 almshouses, still in use today, were funded by local businessman William Penny, who in 1720 left £700 for the 'oasis' to be built, 'to house elderly men of modest means'. The 10 small single 'bed sits', and one double, continue to accommodate a dozen locals, with one cottage left for a warden. The whole place has a communal feel, complete with bench seat overlooking the garden.

The small chapel, with its beautiful stained-glass window and oak panelling surround, holds services regularly for residents, their families and friends, and trustees of the charity that administers the site. It also served as a Bluecoats school for the sons of local craftsmen, and led ultimately to a school for girls.

The whole enterprise was well thought out by Penny, who was Mayor of Lancaster no less than three times. He came up with the idea of a perpetual source of funding for the almshouses by building the Assembly Rooms next door on King Street, as the A6 is known in this section of the city. The revenue raised through balls, concerts and meetings – mainly attended by Lancaster's elite – was used to support the almshouses. It was a neat way to include all stratum of society. In the early 20th century, a road widening scheme for King Street threatened the almshouses, but in the end, two cottages were demolished, as was part of the chapel, with two new cottages being built next door.

Address King Street, Lancaster, LA1 1JN | Getting there From Lancaster Castle, a four-minute walk down Lancaster Hill | Hours Daytime in the courtyard, year round | Tip The adjacent Grade II-listed Assembly Rooms now hosts an eclectic mix of stalls, selling vintage clothes, fancy dress, jewellery, Chinese crafts and pre-owned books (www.lancaster.gov.uk/assemblyrooms).

73 Plover Scar Lighthouse
A flashy and illuminating landmark

There's something quite riveting and alluring about a lighthouse: the imagination runs riot with thoughts of seafaring excitement. Danger on the ocean waves, contrasting with the prospect of a safe home-coming: it's all there as you look out on any lighthouse. And so is the case with Plover Scar Lighthouse, a sturdy, stone-built beacon that has guided vessels into the River Lune estuary since 1847. There it stands, just off the south side of the estuary at Cockersands, a few miles down river from the Port of Lancaster and Glasson Dock. On a benign day in high summer, all looks calm as you gaze out at More-cambe Bay and the Irish Sea beyond. But in a winter storm, with the sou'westerlies raging, it's a different story.

Plover Scar is what they call a 'front range' lighthouse, stand-ing 700 metres out from the 'back range' beacon, the old, on-shore Cockersands Lighthouse, which was demolished. Plover is still functioning, and until 1951 was manned, before being automated. The lighthouse used to be surrounded by what's called a wattle fishing trap, or baulk, which would supply fish for the keepers. The lighthouse itself has a stone-block base, then a white-painted sec-tion, with the light on top, and a weather vane above. It's possible to walk on the rocks and shingle to the lighthouse and back, but be wary of the tides.

One vital necessity remains in the channel – the huge red and green buoys that mark the narrow, central channel of the Lune, test-ing the observer's knowledge that red is for port, and that you always pass the port to the left. With Glasson Dock still being a working port on the southern bank of the Lune, both the buoys and the light-house are still required as navigational aids. Since the Lune channel is subject to change, access for shipping to Glasson is permitted only around high tide, when the dock gates are opened. Embarrassingly, the lighthouse was struck by a vessel in 2016, and needed renovation.

Address LA2 OA2 | Getting there By car from Cockerham Village, go north on the B 5272, then right to the coast on Moss Lane, signposted to Cockerham Sands. On foot, head north along the coastal path, with Cockersands Abbey on your right; check tides at www.tidetimes.co.uk | Tip Wallings Ice Cream has been served by three generations of the family farm on Garstang Road, near Cockerham Village, just five miles away (www.wallings.co.uk).

74 _ The Praying Shell
Sculptor's premonition of cockling tragedy?

Call it an uncanny premonition if you will, but although the evocative sculpture *The Praying Shell* looks out to sea at the very spot where 23 Chinese cocklers lost their lives in Morecambe Bay, the limestone carving was put there three months beforehand. The kneeling figure, hands together in prayer, would seem to be the perfect tribute to the cocklers who drowned in such heart-rending circumstances. That was on the evening of 5 February, 2004, when the fast, incoming tide cut them off in the darkness, claiming the lives of the illegal immigrants put to work in the bay by irresponsible gang-masters.

Yet Lancashire artist Anthony Padgett had designed the limestone figure well before the tragedy occurred, his work being officially unveiled in its cliff-top position the previous November. The sculpture was intended to inspire walkers on the coastal path, but uncannily made reference to cockling. Anthony revealed at the time that the sculpting's symbolism was 'to parallel humanity's openness to a larger dimension, and the way cockle shells open as the tide comes in'.

Even without conjecture that the sculpture could represent a premonition, the stark facts remain. The poverty-stricken immigrants were brought to Liverpool inside lorry containers, then made to go out in to Morecambe Bay without any experience, guidance, or safety measures in place. As darkness fell, the tide swept in, 'faster than a galloping horse', and drowned the helpless cocklers. At the subsequent trial, a survivor testified that the leader of the group had made a mistake about the tide times, and it was revealed that 14 others were thought to have made it ashore. The Chinese gang-masters were given lengthy prison sentences, but the lessons remain: the bay is no place for amateurs, the unwary, or the unprepared, and even experienced local cocklers have moments of drama.

Address Red Bank Farm, The Shore, Bolton-le-Sands, Carnforth, LA5 8JR | Getting there Head south from Bolton-le-Sands, turn right into St Michael's Lane, then left along The Shore; walk through the farmyard, over the stile into a sea-facing field; sculpture looks out to sea. Same overall route by foot. | Hours Daylight all year round | Tip After a possible windswept and reflective experience by the sculpture, the farm has a cosy café called Archer's.

75 Promenade Station
All change for a new Platform

It's always heartening to see something that's side-lined find a new lease of life. The Platform entertainment centre in Morecambe, and the Station pub and eatery next door, are two perfect examples. Once the grand railway entrance to what used to be a vibrant and popular resort, Morecambe's Promenade Station spilled out thousands of holidaymakers and day excursion visitors right there on the seafront.

From its Edwardian heyday – it opened in 1907 – right through to the 1960s and early 1970s, in they flocked. Cotton workers from Lancashire's towns and cities, along with wool mill operatives from West Yorkshire, and families from the industrial heartlands of Glasgow all beat a path to Morecambe. Until, that is, the advent of the package holidays abroad, which had everyone singing 'Viva España'!

Morecambe's railway line once ran across the seafront Promenade and straight on to the Stone Jetty, built in 1853 as a wharf and terminal for ferry passengers and cargo. Hard to believe that coal and coke was sent out to Ireland, with passengers taking ferries to Dublin, Northern Ireland, the Isle of Man and even Scotland – all before Heysham's deep water port was built.

The Promenade Station survived the Beeching axe in the 1960s, but after a small, new station was built nearer to the town centre, the 'Prom' closed in 1994. However, it was sympathetically restored and opened as a major entertainment centre for concerts, dances and events. The adjoining Station pub next door is quite a venue too: its old wooden bar and decor harks back to the old waiting rooms, divided in its time into first and second class, which angered passengers, who felt aggrieved at being segregated. On the walls are vintage railway signs, which adds to the charm of the place. The Platform also houses Morecambe's Visitor Centre, another good use of this old, iconic building.

Address Marine Road West, Morecambe, LA4 4DB | **Getting there** Four-minute walk from Morecambe railway station down Central Drive to Marine Road West | **Hours** Mon – Sat 10am – 4pm | **Tip** The Stone Jetty Café is in the old railway terminus from the days when trains took passengers to the waiting ferries, and freight trains to the dockside.

76 The Radical Steps

Peaceful solution solves pathway problem

It was a radical solution to a radical problem, from a radical thinker. The problem for political firebrand Dr Francis Pearson was that people would walk straight through his garden because it was deemed a public right of way. So he came up with a plan to divert the pathway down a huge flight of stone flag steps that took people on a more direct route to the river bank, way down below his garden on the edge of Kirkby Lonsdale, Naturally, there was opposition, but he constructed them and people used them. They soon became known as the Radical Steps, and they still are to this day.

Originally, there were 46 steps, with 11 landing viewpoints, allowing walkers to admire the views of the surrounding hills and the River Lune, which is fast flowing at this point, 15 miles upstream from the centre of Lancaster. Today, with the landings taken out, there are 86 steps to take you from the edge of St Mary's Churchyard, which is just a short walk from the famous Ruskin's View overlooking the bend of the Lune and out on to the fells of Middleton, Barbon and Leek in the distance.

The steps are part of a three-mile circular walk that takes walkers along the river bank, past a small community of riverside mills dating back to the 18th and 19th centuries and on to Devil's Bridge (see ch. 21), before the long lane back up to town. The former industrial area half way along the route is still linked to the town above by Mill Brow, a steep lane that runs from the river to Market Street in 'KL', as the town is known locally. The area was once the industrial heart of Kirkby Lonsdale, with a number of water-powered mills producing woollen goods and bobbins, as well as snuff. In addition, much of the town's traffic went down the brow, and alongside the river, before crossing Devil's Bridge. Once there, today's walkers can turn right and head up a steep slope back to town. The Radical Steps are 'a steep challenge,' with care advised in the wet.

Address LA6 2FT | **Getting there** From Kirkby Lonsdale's Market Square, follow Main Street to Church Street and into St Mary's Churchyard. Head diagonally across, following signs towards Ruskin's View. The Radical Steps are on your right. | **Hours** Always accessible | **Tip** Just off Market Square at 29 Main Street, is an attraction in Kirkby Lonsdale's Tourist Information Centre: it's the former bank building's vault, where visitors are introduced to historical figures associated with 'KL' – from Ruskin to Turner, from J. M. Barrie, of *Peter Pan* fame, to a wartime evacuee who grew to love the town. It's quite a spectacle, and free!

77 _ Richard Owen Memorial

Terrible lizards, terrible man

A frieze on Lancaster's statue of Queen Victoria has scientists Richard Owen and Charles Darwin next to each other – the only time that happened. They were hardly bosom buddies, to say the least. Lancaster-born Owen had undoubted talents, and was responsible for coining the term 'dinosaur', after the Greek for 'deinos' – meaning 'fearfully great' or 'terrible' – and 'sauros' meaning 'lizard'. He was also the prime mover behind the setting up of London's prestigious Natural History Museum, and his statue graced the main hall, until it was replaced by that of Darwin in 2009.

Such a shame that Owen apparently gained an unwanted reputation for taking credit for the findings of others, with added claims that he was malicious, dishonest and hateful. He was thoroughly disliked by many of his fellow scientists, with Darwin going on record as saying about Owen: 'I will carefully cherish my hatred and contempt to the last of my days.' In addition, an Oxford professor said pithily: 'Pity a man so talented could be so dastardly and envious.' Strong stuff, even by academic standards! Little wonder he was voted off the councils of the Royal Society and the Zoological Society.

Owen, son of a Lancaster merchant who traded with the West Indies, went to Lancaster Royal Grammar School, and ultimately became a favourite of Queen Victoria, who knighted him for his scientific contribution. He was educated to a high degree in Edinburgh and London, was an outstanding naturalist, and had a remarkable ability to interpret fossils. As such, he was a natural to place on the scientific section of the frieze on the Queen Victoria Memorial in Dalton Square, diagonally opposite to the Owens' home. This stood at the entrance to Common Garden Street but is now demolished. An explanatory mural is on the neighbouring building, and a plaque honours him at his former school.

Address Dalton Square, Lancaster, LA1 1PJ | Getting there Two-minute walk from Nelson Street car park | Hours Public access all year round | Tip Raise a glass to 'the dinosaur man' at Wetherspoon's city centre pub, the Sir Richard Owen (4 Spring Garden Street).

78 Rocking Horse Shop Sign
Things looking up for shop signs of Lancaster

The old rocking horse is a much-loved shop sign in Lancaster, but it so nearly fell at the last hurdle. For decades the beautifully-constructed equine sign was positioned above the entrance to Lawson's Toy Shop on New Street in Lancaster's shopping area, delighting children and parents alike. However, in 2014, with Lawson's long gone, and a burger bar establishment having taken its place, the decision was made to remove the famous white rocking horse, and its red rockers: the wood was rotting, the joints were disintegrating, and there was real danger of the rocking horse falling on passers-by. Naturally, there was a hue and cry regarding this 'lost treasure', and various bodies stepped up to the plate, including Lancaster's Business Improvement District. The aim was simple: rescue the horse and get it back in the running.

Local designer James Mackie was the man charged with the task, but this was no mean feat, considering the horse's age, condition, size and weight. Much of the woodwork had to be replaced, a new hip sorted out, a real horse's hair tail and mane attached, not to mention the task of sanding and gilding. A new 'fairy tale look' was achieved, and the rocking horse was reinstated. Thereafter, a restaurant moved in, calling itself the 'Rocking Horse Chinese', and although the establishment closed down as a result of the COVID-19 pandemic, the horse still rides high above the shop front.

Another surviving shop sign in Lancaster is the large pestle and mortar on the wall above the Well Chemist's Shop in King Street, with both the old toy shop and the pharmacy having green plaques into the bargain. The pawnbroker on Ffrances Passage (see ch. 10) has the traditional sign of three golden balls, and a large teapot/kettle and a golden canister from other shop fronts are preserved in Lancaster City Museum in Market Square. It offers a great insight into Lancaster's history – and it's free.

Address 8 New Street, Lancaster, LA1 1EG | Getting there Three-minute walk from Lancaster bus station or a five-minute walk from Lancaster railway station | Hours Accessible all year round | Tip Four miles along Ashton Road from Lancaster is a remarkable pub sign: a stork with wings outstretched as it takes off from the exterior wall of the Stork Hotel in the hamlet of Conder Green.

79 __ Roman Remains
They didn't 'wery' about the wall

The name Wery Wall is not only unusual, it's an enigmatic clue to Lancaster's Roman past. It may appear to be little more than a pile of old stones, but it's the remaining fragment of Lancaster's ancient Roman fortress, and adjacent to the remains of a Roman bathhouse. That was well before the medieval bastion of Lancaster Castle was built, of course. However, the Roman legacy lives on: the Roman name for 'Fort on the Lune' – Lancestra – became Lancaster, and survives to this day. So what can be seen of the Roman presence? This is, in effect, the final remains of the defensive walls built over a period from AD 71, when the Romans conquered the North of England, to around AD 340. And what of that tongue-twisting name?

The term 'Wery Wall' is thought to have come from the Anglo-Saxons, who arrived after the Roman legions quit Britain. The word 'werian' means 'to defend', thus making the term 'defensive wall'. Over time, the abbreviated phrase stuck, even though the wall of Caesar's rule fell into ruins, and became the victim of stone robbers. As they say in Downtown Lancaster: 'One man's defensive wall is another man's gable end.'

All that is left for us to see is a huge block of stones by the side of the equally-sparse remains of the bathhouse; even so, it is still Grade II-listed. Interestingly, Lancaster Council asked Oxford Archaeological North for advice on how best to preserve these two small but significant fragments of the Roman Empire in Britain. Hopefully, they gave the council a tongue bashing for allowing a concrete monstrosity of a wall to be built in such close proximity back in the 1970s. The term 'institutionalised vandalism' springs to mind. Not that the Romans left everything untouched. It's estimated that three or four separate forts were built on roughly the same area, each 'vandalising' the previous one.

Address Vicarage Fields below Lancaster Priory, behind the castle | **Getting there** The remains are half-way along a path that runs from the Priory Churchyard to the Lune quayside, and can be entered from either end: 13, Damside, LA1 1UZ, or from the Priory, LA1 1YZ | **Hours** Daylight all year round | **Tip** Visit Lancaster City Museum in the Old Town Hall in Market Square to see the remarkable Roman Cavalry Tombstone, dating from 100 AD, and discovered on a Lancaster building site.

80___Royal Kings Arms

Dickens of a story with the bride's ghost

Charles Dickens never missed a trick when it came to material, and Lancaster gave it to him on a plate. His story *The Ghost in the Bride's Chamber* was based on a poisoner who killed his wife while staying at Lancaster's Royal Kings Arms, near Lancaster Castle. Dickens made his visit to the hotel en route to the Lake District just two weeks after the poisoner was hanged in 1857, when the story was still on everyone's lips. It had everything: the motive of money; a public hanging with a crowd of more than 8,000; the haunting of the room where the bride died. It even kick-started the hotel custom of serving 'bride's cake' to guests after their dinner. Dickens savoured it all, including the cake, and wrote the story, even claiming that he had felt the presence of the bride's ghost in the room where he stayed.

The poisoner was in fact Edward Hardman, a shoemaker from the Lancashire town of Chorley. He had joined several 'burial clubs', which paid out handsomely when the paying member had a bereavement. When it was discovered that he had purchased a large amount of arsenic just before his wife's death, her body was exhumed and examined, to discover she was the victim of arsenic poisoning. Although Dickens was on his way to the Lake District with his friend and writing colleague, Wilkie Collins, he couldn't resist the murder story with a ghostly twist.

Today's Royal Kings Arms is still a high-class hotel, though very different from the original 17th-century coaching inn, just off the main route north to Scotland. It was rebuilt after a fire in 1879, but the Dickens' Room, with its four-poster bed, is still a favourite, especially for newly-married couples! Perhaps more surprisingly, the original hotel was owned by King Louis XIV of France, who installed tapestries designed by Rubens. The reason for this French connection remains a mystery.

Address 75 Market Street, Lancaster, LA1 1JG, www.royalkingsarmshotel.co.uk | **Getting there** Three-minute walk from Lancaster station; parking available in nearby Dallas Road Car Park | **Hours** Always accessible | **Tip** You can sleep in a four-poster double bed in the Dickens Room where the author stayed; there's also the hotel's Crypt, which is a classy cocktail lounge, wine bar and eatery.

81 The Ruskin

'Love and skill working together – a masterpiece'

It's quite a feather in the cap for Lancaster to have the world's largest collection of works by the acclaimed John Ruskin, the master critic, writer, environmentalist and social thinker of the 19th century. But there on the campus of Lancaster University is a simply magnificent, state-of-the-art building that houses Ruskin's treasure trove. Thousands of paintings, diagrams, letters, articles and photographs have been curated in The Ruskin, which works jointly with Brantwood, Ruskin's home for 38 years, on the banks of Coniston Water in the Lake District, and just an hour's drive from Lancaster.

It makes sense to combine their firepower to keep the torch burning for one of the most advanced and radical thinkers of his age. He was ahead of his time in articulating the fact that industry was poisoning and polluting the atmosphere, and one of the earliest advocates of the danger of climate change and ultimately of global warming.

The Ruskin is in fact a library, museum and research centre, and although its activities were curtailed and disrupted by the COVID-19 pandemic, it remained open to the public for exhibitions, talks, performances and creative workshops, some held in Lancaster Castle. As well as an academic centre of excellence, the staff have an outreach policy to help local schools and colleges, representing a consciousness of communal benefit and duty that is worthy of the great man himself.

As a friend and admirer of J. M. W. Turner, who pushed the barriers of art in his time, you feel sure that Ruskin would have approved of the stylish yet functional museum that was designed by the award-winning, modernist architect Richard MacCormac. Outside, the university is developing a garden worthy of Ruskin, a space that is 'beautiful, peaceful and fruitful', and that has a shelter for an outdoor classroom or sitting space.

Address Bailrigg, Lancaster University, LA1 4YH, www.lancaster.ac.uk/news/the-ruskin-whitehouse-collection-1, the-ruskin@lancaster.ac.uk | Getting there By car, take M 6 J 33, follow signs for Lancaster, take the A 6 north through Galgate; bus 4 and 4X every half hour Mon – Sat from Lancaster railway station | Hours Weekdays 10am – 4pm | Tip While on the campus, visit the Peter Scott Gallery. Not named after the wildlife expert of Slimbridge fame, but a local benefactor and philanthropist. The focus is on 20th-century prints and paintings, Pilkington ceramics, plus Chinese and Japanese art.

82 Seabird Sculptures
Tern for the better on Morecambe Prom

A series of huge steel razorbills, cormorants and gannets perch on massive rocks, and a flock of metal oyster catchers in flight adorn metal structures on Morecambe's seafront Promenade. The 'Prom' – all five miles of it – was rebuilt using a government grant for coastal protection. It was a touch of genius all round, proclaiming that the run-down resort was on its way back. And the finishing touch was the adornment of the Prom and the revamped Old Stone Jetty with the birds of the bay. The Tern Project, named after the tern wading bird, put the town back in touch with its vast seascape, covering 120 square miles. It was a massive boost in local pride, and the combination of form, function and flair would have made William Morris proud. Certainly, the Queen loved it as she officially opened the project.

As part of the scheme, vehicle roundabouts in the town also display the huge public art works – with a large gannet sculpture here and a cormorant there, tuning into the theme of savouring Morecambe Bay's rich birdlife. Towards the northern end of the promenade is a purposefully-rusting art work of the mountains and hills across the bay. Three ranges overlap, with Warton Crag and Arnside marked on the first, the Lakeland fells on the second, and Lake District mountains such as Hellvelyn on the more distant range.

The Tern Project not only gives a great deal of joy to visitors and locals alike, but the coastal regeneration scheme came to the rescue of a resort urgently in need of repair and reinvention, beginning in the mid-1990s and continuing to this day. Lancaster Council saw it all as 'a gorgeous opportunity' to kick start and to give a natural focus to the refurbishment programme. It provided a backcloth to inspire the 2006 regeneration of the Art Deco Midland Hotel, and now the prospect of an Eden Project North. The excitement mounts.

Address Stone jetty area, Morecambe, LA4 4NJ | Getting there Seven-minute walk from Morecambe railway station; behind the Midland is the Stone Jetty and many of the bird sculptures | Tip The Stone Jetty is a delight in itself. The imaginatively and creatively refurbished walkway out into the bay has a small lighthouse at the end, next to an interesting café. Strange to think that this was once a cargo and passenger pier, and at one time a ship scrapyard!

83 _ Settlement of Stydd

A disguised church, almshouses and the Holy Land

It's a place with three distinct buildings – a disguised church, a one-time hospital base for pilgrims to the Holy Land, and the most elaborately-designed almshouses you'll ever see. With stories about the involvement of Crusading religious order the Knights Hospitaller, the whole story could come straight out of Dan Brown's intriguing thriller *The Da Vinci Code*.

Tucked away, deliberately out of sight near the Ribble Valley village of Ribchester, is a one-time discreet Catholic 'hideaway' called the settlement of Stydd. There, can be found the 18th-century RC Church of St Peter and St Paul, an early 'barn church', built to look like a farmer's barn to disguise its true purpose during times when Catholics were forbidden to have public places for worship. Next to the church can be found Stydd Almshouses, built by local Catholic landowner John Shireburn, whose family were prime movers behind the nearby Jesuit citadel of Stonyhurst College.

The almshouses, built in 1728, incorporate an amazing concoction of styles. The two-storey building has a gallery, or arcade, for the upper floor residents, with five bays – the middle three in stone, the outer bays in brick. In the centre is a flight of fanned steps, leading from the first-floor arcade. The almshouses are still in use, having been restored in 1990, with the resulting flats now being administered by a housing association.

Just up the road is the third building, the one with the exotic connections with pilgrimages to the Holy Land. St Saviour's Church, now linked with St Wilfrid's CofE Church in Ribchester, was originally associated with the Knights Hospitallers, who ran pilgrims' hospitals in the Middle East back in the 11th and 12th centuries. In Stydd, they are said to have run either a hospital for the sick, a hostel for pilgrims, or a hospice for the terminally ill. Unusually, the church is austere, with flagged floor and whitewashed walls.

Address Stydd Lane, Stydd, Ribchester, PR3 3YQ | Getting there By car, 45 minutes from Lancaster via the M 6, or an hour via the Trough of Bowland, through Dunsop Bridge and Chipping | Hours Accessible during daylight hours | Tip Nearby Stydd Gardens in Stoneygate Lane is a garden centre with a difference. It has a nursery specialising in old-fashioned roses, a restaurant, café and tearooms inside a giant glasshouse, and a host of creative small businesses, such as vintage lighting, a herb specialist, and a wine merchant (www.stydd.com).

84 Sherlock Holmes' School
An Elementary Connection, my dear Conan Doyle

No doubt the pupils of Stonyhurst College frighten each other with tales about a huge and fearsome hound coming down from the Lancashire moors at night. The horrific prospect is something straight out of Sir Arthur Conan Doyle's novella *The Hounds of the Baskervilles*, which is not that surprising: after all, he was a pupil himself from the age of nine onwards, and his desk can still be seen. Conan Doyle spent seven years at Stonyhurst, the Jesuit-run college in the heart of the Ribble Valley, just 45 minutes from Lancaster. The influence of that time in the author's life is clearly evident in place names and characters in his celebrated books about the legendary detective, Sherlock Holmes.

Fellow pupils included a Sherlock, and the Moriarty twins, one of whom was fiendishly clever. Enter the arch criminal and manipulator, Professor Moriarty, who pitted his wits and intelligence against that of Holmes. Baskerville Hall is obviously Stonyhurst, with its 'Dark Walk' becoming The Yew Alley, in which Sir Charles Baskerville is literally frightened to death by the hound. No doubt the attributes given to the inspirational detective were learned by Conan Doyle through the rigours of a Jesuit-based education. The practice of observation, logical reasoning, deduction and forensic science became Holmes' hallmarks. His famous phrases live on, such as 'To a great mind, nothing is little' and 'It is my business to know what other people do not know.' However, the most commonly used one – 'Elementary, my dear Watson' – was not invented by Conan Doyle, but was ascribed to Holmes by P. J. Wodehouse, then popularised in films.

More conventionally, another pupil was innovative poet Gerard Manley Hopkins, who went on to become a Jesuit Priest. A Catholic convert, he went to Stonyhurst for philosophy studies and to take his Jesuitical vows of piety, chastity and poverty.

Address Stonyhurst College, Clitheroe, BB7 9PZ, +44 (0)1254 826 345, www.stonyhurst.ac.uk |
Getting there By car, from M 6 J 32, take the B 5269 and B 6243 to your destination near
Hurst Green | Hours Open days or by request | Tip Bashall Barn, just a 10-minute drive
away, is a farm-based complex with a café, restaurant and shop, and delicious home-made
products in the ice cream parlour.

85 _ *SHIP* Sculpture

The art of looking forward and back

It's hardly ready to sail the Seven Seas, but the rusting Viking long-ship above Heysham's Half Moon Bay is meant to be symbolic. It's stunningly beautiful into the bargain. The sheer simplicity of the huge, free-standing artwork by Anna Gillespie, called *SHIP*, gives joy to all who pass by it on the path to Heysham Headland. It also makes you think. There it stands in all its majesty – the frame of a Viking longboat, with two male figures on board. On high, one looks forward from the prow, the other looks back from the stern.

The one 'forard' faces Heysham Port, with all its comings and goings, while the one to the rear looks towards the ancient ruins of St Patrick's Chapel on Heysham Headland, a place where Viking and Roman settlers arrived. The artwork reflects the fact that Heysham has long been a point of arrival and departure. *SHIP* also celebrates Morecambe Bay's landscape and maritime heritage, and reflects the importance of the sea in shaping the character of the area. It looks forward to the 'new' in the gigantic shape of Heysham's two nuclear power plants (see ch. 69), while musing over its past glories on the headland to the rear. Both the nuclear industry and the Viking invasions present that back-of-the-mind element of potential danger.

The artist also symbolically positioned her artwork on the bound-ary between land and sea, benefitting from dramatic backdrops of the tides, the shifting sands and channels, the distant horizon, and the stunning coastal sunsets. But why no woman on board *SHIP*? Anna says candidly: 'If you had a man and a woman on the bow and stern of the ship, it would have been like a relationship where they were sitting back to back – it didn't seem right. I hope at some point I can do another sculpture to balance it out.' *SHIP* was commissioned by the Morecambe Bay Partnership as part of the Headlands to Head-space project.

Address Half Moon Bay, Heysham, LA3 2LA | Getting there From St Patrick's Chapel on Heysham Head, a 20-minute walk along Heysham Coastal Line pathway; by car, from Heysham Main Street, turn right on Barrows Lane, then right along Smithy Lane to Half Moon Bay Car Park | Hours Always accessible | Tip Sit and savour the sculpture, the pathway to Heysham Headland and the seafront of Half Moon Bay over a cuppa and a cake at the friendly Half Moon Café.

86 Slave Shame Memorial

Captured Africans remembered on Lancaster quay

It's not immediately apparent, but the *Captured Africans* sculpture on Lancaster's quayside depicts the city's involvement in the slave trade. At first sight, it's not obvious that the six rectangular Perspex blocks, one on top of the other, are meant to represent the decks of a vessel taking captured Africans across the Atlantic to the West Indies. Upon each block is written the different commodities brought back to Lancaster: wealth is uppermost, with other blocks representing cotton, rum, mahogany, sugar – and slaves. The stainless steel column lists 200 ships that went out from Lancaster, and the number of slaves seized on the West African coast.

The sculpture, by Kevin Dalton-Johnson, reveals that between 1750 and 1790 alone, Lancaster merchants were responsible for the forced transportation of around 29,000 African men, women and children across the Atlantic. Rarely was a slave actually brought to Lancaster, but the size and magnificence of the old Customs House – now Lancaster Maritime Museum – on St George's Quay, indicates the magnitude of the triangular trade. The city's Georgian buildings also reflect the wealth of historic residents.

When the Black Lives Matter movement took off in 2020, Lancaster was not immune. Just a couple of days after the toppling of the statue of Bristol slave trader Edward Colston, the memorial to the Rawlinson slave-trading family in Lancaster was targeted. The memorial in the Priory Church graveyard was spray painted in red with the words 'Slave Trader'. There was also a call to rename the former 18th-century sugar boiling plant 'The Sugarhouse', which is now a nightclub, as its original operation was based on plantation-grown sugar cane. It was decided by Lancaster University's Students' Union, which runs the club, to keep the name but to increase awareness of the city's slave trade past. Kevin Dalton-Johnson's work is part of the Slave Trade Arts Memorial Project.

Address Near Millennium Bridge on Damside Street, LA1 1AY | Getting there Five-minute walk from Lancaster bus station; by car, through Lancaster's one-way, north-bound A 6, turning left into Damside Street at foot of hill | Hours Always accessible | Tip A stroll along St George's Quay gives a feel for Lancaster's historic port trade – the huge warehouses, the mooring points for tall ships, ancient pubs, and the Customs House itself.

87 Snatchems and Catchems

Lune-acy of Lancaster's press gangs

The names 'Snatchems' and 'Catchems' are so evocative, and live on to this day as place names on the north bank of the River Lune. They reveal the age-old practice of able-bodied men being forced into service on ocean-going merchant vessels. It was an ever-present threat, from the quayside pubs in Lancaster and the riverside haunts downstream, on the way to the Atlantic Ocean. Lancaster's key target pub was the Three Mariners, at the eastern end of St George's Quay, and at the foot of Castle Hill. The other target was the one-time Golden Ball, to be found on the northern bank of the Lune, on the riverside road to Sunderland Point. The latter was always known as 'Snatchems', and a place nearby was called 'Catchems', the names living on three centuries after the press gang activity began in the 18th century.

The practice may not have been as systematic as that of the Royal Navy, but the consequences for individuals and their families were just as dramatic and devastating. The suddenness of the operation could be brutal, both in manner and execution. A group of sailors would enter the riverside pubs in Lancaster, ostensibly to take a drink before sailing. They would target victims, ply them with ale, then spirit them aboard their vessel, before sailing off on the high tide. If they were still men short, they would take a small boat to the Golden Ball and 'top up' with local farm workers.

Once the victims came round, the sailing ship would be miles out at sea, en route to West Africa to take slaves across the Atlantic to the West Indies, on the second leg of the lucrative 'Triangular Trade'. It would be many months before they would return to Lancaster, fully laden with rum, sugar or hardwood on the third leg of their journey. At least the captive seamen were fed and watered, which was so often not the case with families left behind without the main breadwinner.

Address Three Mariners, Bridge Lane, Lancaster, LA1 1EE | **Getting there** 10-minute walk from the Lancaster railway station, or 3-minute walk from Lancaster bus station; limited free parking available along the quayside, or use the adjacent 'Parksafe' | **Hours** Daily 11am–11pm | **Tip** The pub 'cellar' is on the first floor, to avoid quarrying into the hard rock strata below and any flood risk, should the nearby River Lune overflow; fortunately, the pub's ground floor is just above the danger zone.

88_ Soul Bowl

Strike it lucky with a ten-pin tonic

If the ancient game of outdoor bowls is considered a gentleman's sport, then indoor ten-pin bowling is the modern alternative with an American vibe, and is a very popular pastime among residents and visitors to Morecambe – especially on those rainy days! As a result, the resort has its very own 'traditional' ten-pin bowling alley called Soul Bowl, which has 10 lanes – or alleys – fashioned from wood. It's a noisy spectacle when someone scores a 'strike', a single ball knocking down all 10 pins – what better way to spend a couple of hours, engaged in a little competitive exercise? But although the game is competitive, no one gets hurt – unless you forget to let go of the ball, which can weigh up to 16 pounds, as you attempt to hurl it down the 60-foot lane towards the 'V' of pins at the far end.

Although ten-pin bowling is associated strongly with America, the game was invented by German peasants who called it 'kegeling'. This has nothing to do with the modern pelvic muscle control exercises invented by Arnold Henry Kegel, but an original, nine-pin game that was popular in Europe. In America, in the 1830s, there was moral panic around the suggestion that nine-pin bowls had become associated with gambling and organised crime, so to get around the resultant outlawing legislation, ten-pin bowling was invented!

Soul Bowl has much to commend it, offering both games and food. There are pool tables and a set of fussball – (table football) games, which are always popular. There's also 'lane food' available, and the Vista Soul Bar and Kitchen serves Italian-style cuisine in a restaurant setting, complete with beautiful views out over Morecambe Bay, to be savoured over cocktails and its range of gins. Soul Bowl can be found right on the seafront, on the opposite side of the road from the Midland Hotel and Eric Morecambe's 'Bring Me Sunshine' statue.

Address 210 Marine Road Central, Morecambe, LA4 4BU | **Getting there** Four-minute walk from Morecambe railway station | **Hours** Mon–Thu 9am–11pm, Fri & Sat 9–1.30am, Sun 9am–10pm | **Tip** Happy Mount Park is a free-entry public park with a huge offering, from Crown Green bowls to pitch and putt, swing boats to trampolines, from a splash park to a children's park.

89__Star Café Mural

Mega-market memorial to a lost child

The Star Café is the sort of place where you eat dinner at mid-day – definitely not lunch! As you tuck into steak pie, chips and two veg, you can celebrate 'all that's good in Morecambe'. That's how artist Bob Pickersgill describes the mural he painted across an entire wall of the Star Café in the Festival Market. The mural, a talking point for locals and visitors alike since it first appeared in 2017, is dedicated to the café owner's son, Nikki, who died aged just 13.

The brightly-coloured wall painting features a reproduction of the celebrated Eric Gill mural from the foyer of The Midland Hotel, and the equally-celebrated Eric Ravilious mural in the hotel's Rotunda Bar. A song-and-dance couple, the Eric Morecambe Statue, and the comedian's Rolls-Royce car are also depicted. The seafront Clock Tower is featured, as well as the last two Morecambe shrimping boats, and the attendant wild birds of the Bay. There are children playing with a beach ball on the sands, off-shore yachting, and a nod to the great day of holiday entertainment, highlighted by the sign *Vintage by the Sea* – the name of a very successful and enjoyable two-day festival put on by the Morecambe-born designer, Wayne Hemingway.

Artist Bob Pickersgill studied at Liverpool School of Art and trained as a sign writer, before ultimately moving to Morecambe. As a user of the café, he came up with the idea of the mural, to create interest on a huge blank wall, while also pleasing the customers. Bob is gaining quite a reputation for his murals, following the launch of his first one at Carnforth Railway Station, north of Morecambe: it depicts a steam train and vintage buses, in keeping with the heritage centre there. Other noteable ventures include a mural of actress Dame Thora Hird, Morecambe's most famous daughter, and one of 'Auntie Wainwright,' who starred in the TV series *Last of the Summer Wine*.

Address Off Central Drive near the seafront roundabout by The Platform, Morecambe, LA4 4DW | Getting there By car, parking is available off Marine Road Central, directly opposite the Midland Hotel | Hours Apr–Sep Tue, Thu, Sat, Sun 9am–5pm, Oct–Mar 9am–4.30pm | Tip Between the market and the car park is a pathway made up of poems, jokes and quotes by famous authors, musicians, entertainers and artists; it's part of Morecambe's Tern Project, a trail with sculptures and novelties.

90 Storey Institute

Stunning spectacle of Lancaster's stained glass

The stained-glass window in Lancaster's Storey Institute is not only a stunning piece of craftsmanship, it also has a highly unusual feature. The depiction of famous historical names in the world of literature, music, art and architecture is impressive enough, but the whole piece is on a curve. That's something not easily achieved, and rarely seen.

Being on the first floor of the impressive, city-centre building known simply as 'The Storey', the light shines through this hidden gem, illuminating the names chosen by local oilcloth manufacturer and philanthropist, Sir Thomas Storey. His admiration extended to Wren, Handel, Bennett and Chaucer: obviously he was a man of some taste, as well as wide-ranging vision for his home city. Storey placed high value on education, and created the original institute as a centre for technical, scientific and artistic innovation. In particular, he wanted young people to have a better chance than their parents, and offered the facilities for self-help. The premises were built to honour Queen Victoria's Golden Jubilee in 1897, and within two years of opening, it was exhibiting works by Gainsborough, Constable and Canaletto. Today, the council-owned 'hub' for businesses, events, exhibitions and meetings is called simply 'The Storey' in grateful recognition.

In the 19th and 20th centuries, Lancaster had built a growing reputation for stained-glass art work, with three firms at the cutting edge of design and workmanship. Shrigley and Hunt, the company responsible for the Storey commission, was based in Castle Street and often favoured a pre-Raphaelite style; Abbott and Company was more modernist, and responsible for decorative work in inter-war housing; finally, Seward and Company was based in the Music Room Pavilion in Sun Street. All three have work exhibited in Lancaster City Museum in Market Square.

Address Meeting House Lane, Lancaster, LA1 1TH, www.lancaster.gov.uk/sites/
the-storey | Getting there Lancaster station is a short walk away; limited car parking
is free for three hours in Meeting House Lane, but Dallas Car Park is just a short walk
away | Hours Mon–Fri 8.30am–9pm, Sat 9am–6pm | Tip Walk up Castle Hill to the
impressive Lancaster Priory Church, the city's Mother Church, which is on a site that has
seen Christian worship since Saxon times. Much of the Medieval element still stands, with
choir stalls dating back to the 14th century.

91 St Mary's Gates

Unique mechanism for – or by – mysterious WG

Normally, the iron gates of an ancient, architecturally-fascinating church dating back to Norman times, might expect to get second billing, perhaps even third. But the self-closing gates of St Mary's in Kirkby Lonsdale are a fascinating point of interest in their own right. So fascinating that they have been included in a worldwide list of 'Gates of Distinction' – something of a wonder for old West-morland.

Certainly, the gates – two large, central structures, and two smaller ones at each side – are pleasing to the eye, beautifully proportioned, and perfectly functional. But it's the simple and ingenious mechanism that makes them close without human hand that gives them a unique distinction. No-one seems to know whether they were invented as a one-off by 'WG', the name on the iron work, or whether it was WG who made them to order, back in 1823. Whatever the case, it's the hinge and closure that makes the gates great. Quite simply, when one of them is opened, a piece of attached metal rolls up a curved slope on a small metal wheel, which reaches a limit when fully opened, then rolls back automatically due to gravity and the weight of the gate itself. The much-used side gates' mechanisms are well greased and work easily: the large, central ones are somewhat drier, being used only on special occasions. To finalise the structure, a lamp is set high above in an iron loop.

The gates initially cost the princely sum of £43, six shillings, five and three-quarter pence; the cost of restoring them almost 200 years later was over £11,000! Still, they are a joy to behold, up there along-side gates in St Louis on the Mississippi River, the Gate of Ceme-nerio in Spain, the Kabouterhuis Gate in Amsterdam, the Park Hotel gate in Turku, Finland, and the ornate leaf design gate in Millbank Road, Darlington. Eat your heart out, County Durham! A hanging basket of flowers often hangs from the arch to add to the beauty.

Address Church Street, Kirkby Lonsdale, LA6 2AX | Getting there Five-minute walk from Market Square | Hours Always accessible | Tip Look up at the strangely-placed, off-centre public clock on the left side of St Mary's Church tower.

92 Stone Igloo
Capturing a 'hole' new horizon

Visitors to Sunderland Point are baffled by what seems to be a stone-built igloo on the Morecambe Bay shoreline, just north of Sunderland Point on the River Lune estuary. The well-constructed building is intriguing, to say the least. Is it a shelter? Is it an art form? Does it serve a purpose? The answer to all three of these questions is 'yes'.

You can shelter in the head-high construction, should a 'Nor' Wester' be in full force, roaring out of Morecambe Bay. It is also an artful addition to the various sculptures and artworks that are dotted round the Bay, from Ulverston and Brigsteer on the northern coast, right round to Heysham and Sunderland Point in the south. In addition, it has an active use for visitors to the shoreline as a way of feeling a sense of place in quite an unusual manner.

To give the igloo its full scientific name, it is a *camera obscura*, with a pinhole-type aperture in the solid wall on the seaward side, causing the light, and the sight, of the horizon to project on to the opposite wall, on the landward Lancaster side of the structure. Officially, it's called the Horizon Line Chamber, and was the idea of international environmental artist Chris Drury, who was commissioned by the Morecambe Bay Partnership as part of its 'Headlands to Headspace' art project.

Drury, now in his 70s, wanted to create an innovative experience for visitors to the area, providing a self-contained projector for the world outside the 'igloo'. The surrounding sea, the shifting light, and the wildlife all added to its appeal, with his remit being 'to complement, conserve and capture' the experiences. He was helped by master craftsman and stone mason Andrew Mason, and together they created the means of appreciating the big skies, the vast openness and long horizons that are the hallmark of Morecambe Bay. The igloo is adjacent to Little Sambo's Grave (see ch. 60).

Address LA3 3HP | Getting there By car, from Lancaster, take Morecambe Road across the River Lune Bridge, then A 589/Bay Gateway/A 683, turn left on Lancaster Road to Overton, then across the tidal road to Sunderland Point. Access between First Terrace and Second Terrace, LA3 3HR, follow The Lane inland for a five-minute walk to the igloo. | Hours Visit during daylight hours at low tide only – treacherous tidal road: check tide times | Tip Explore the two rows of houses, warehouses and former ale houses alongside the makeshift road by the riverfront at Sunderland Point. There was even a Temperance Hostelry, and today, another artwork, this time in metal, depicting local wildlife.

93 Stonyhurst College

Oliver Cromwell's heavy metal gig at Stonyhurst

Just wearing a suit of armour must have been demanding enough, let alone having to sleep in it. Yet that's precisely what Oliver Cromwell did when he spent the night at Stonyhurst College, the great Jesuit school in the heart of Lancashire's Ribble Valley.

Near the end of the Second English Civil War in 1648, Cromwell's New Model Army was on its way to engage with the Royalists and the Scots near Preston. His 8,500-strong Parliamentarian force had marched across the Pennines from Yorkshire, and when they arrived at Stonyhurst on 16 August, they set up camp for an overnight stay in the college grounds.

As a Protestant fundamentalist, Cromwell was hardly afforded a warm welcome in the midst of high Catholics, in a part of Lancashire that was traditionally a Papal stronghold. Fearing assassination while he slept, Cromwell did not remove his protective armour, and laid out on a refectory table in the centre of the Great Hall. He survived intact, and the next day, his troops made for Walton-le-Dale, near Preston, ready to take on their enemies.

Cromwell's Parliamentarians were outnumbered by the combined forces of the Royalists, loyal to Charles I, and the main Scottish deployment led by the Duke of Hamilton. However, Cromwell out-flanked them from the start: he routed the Scots' advanced guard, before engaging the main contingent the following day, 17 August. The three-day Battle of Preston ended in victory for Cromwell, with the Royalists and Scots bludgeoned into submission.

The rectory table that Cromwell slept on at Stonyhurst remains in the college's Great Hall to this day, acting as a reminder of the Lord Protector's imposed visit. Traditionally, naughty boys at the school were made to sit at the table, presumably to reflect upon their sins as they gazed down at the table where Cromwell had spent an undoubt-edly uncomfortable night.

Address Stonyhurst College, Clitheroe, BB7 9PZ, +44 (0)1254 826345, www.stonyhurst.ac.uk |
Getting there By car, from M 6 J 32 take the B 5269 and B 6243 to your destination near
Hurst Green | Hours Open days or by request; see website for current information on
visiting | Tip Cromwell's Bridge over the River Hodder may be only two metres wide, but
it was robust enough to allow the Lord Protector's 8,500 troops to cross. Its side walls were
dismantled to allow cannons to be taken over – and that is how it remains. Visible from the
nearby B 6243.

94 The Storey Garden

City-centre orchard bears fruit

There's something enchanting and quite magical about a secret garden – and Lancaster has one such hidden gem right in the city centre. The Storey Garden is a walled oasis that is reached through an impressive entrance on Castle Hill, virtually opposite Lancaster Castle. It's an enchanting sanctuary, and the story could be straight out of the book *The Secret Garden* by Manchester-born Frances Hodgson Bennett. In the much-loved classic, a young orphaned girl comes across a locked-up, walled garden that is overgrown and neglected: it all ends well as the garden is brought back to its pristine condition, and the blighted life of the owner also enjoys a new lease of life. In similar fashion, Lancaster's Storey Garden is on its way back, as is the reputation of its original owner, Sir Thomas Storey, the man responsible for the garden back in the late 19th century. He was elected Mayor four times and was responsible for the nearby arts, science and business hub called 'The Storey'.

Part of the original garden has been transformed into an orchard, being laid out in the form of tree branches. The four main branch pathways have four types of fruit tree – apple, cherry, plum and pear, with bronze sculptures of each type on tall pedestals. Many of the trees are rare or endangered, a deliberate act to preserve a wider range of tastes and textures, away from the uniformity that has been seen increasingly in modern times.

Until recently, the garden had become neglected and overgrown, until the Friends of Storey Gardens raised funds for restoration work, putting in the hard hours of maintenance too. Help came from Tate Liverpool and the Henry Moore Trust, both of which invested in the artwork required. Access, on Castle Hill, is through an amazing portico, in Roman Doric style, with two columns supporting a cornice that once graced a private house. Opposite, a flight of Georgian steps is often used for art illustrations.

Address Castle Hill, Lancaster, LA1 1TH, www.storeygardens.org | Getting there
A short walk from Lancaster station; free car parking is available for three hours in Meeting
House Lane, but Dallas Car Park is just a short walk away | **Hours** Mon–Fri, Mar–Oct
10am–4pm, Nov–Feb 10am–3pm | Tip Gresgarth Hall, just six miles up the Lune
Valley near Caton, has an award-winning garden designed by renowned plantswoman
Arabella Lennox-Boyd, who lives there with husband Mark, the area's former MP
(www.arabellalennoxboyd.com).

95 St Peter's Viking Grave
Living high on the hogback in Heysham

When you enter a fully-operational consecrated church, you might not expect to see a historic Viking grave relic on display. Yet there it is, the remarkable 'hogback' grave cover, set in a prominent position in St Peter's Church. The carved, solid stone adornment is in near-perfect condition, and dates back to the 9th century, when the Viking presence was felt on the headland at Heysham. The long, narrow grave cover, shaped like a long, linear hogback ridge, was a Scandinavian introduction to the British Isles, and used to signify the burial of someone of importance at the time. It passed out of fashion in the 11th century when the Norman invasion meant their own customs and control spread north.

Other hogback examples were found in the Glasgow district of Govan, on the south bank of the Clyde, and soon afterwards, the one in Heysham. The hogback was discovered in St Peter's Churchyard sometime between 1807 and 1811, centuries on from when the church was founded in the ninth century. The Heysham hogback is carved from pale-brown millstone grit, and is said to have been found with a skeleton and a spear. It is quite large as examples go, and is much prized both locally and nationally. Measuring almost 206cm long, 28cm wide and 53cm high, it has small carvings of beasts, mammals, birds, a tree, and a human figure.

Of late, the Heysham community has embraced its Viking past. A weekend Viking Festival has been held in July for four consecutive years, though the COVID-19 pandemic meant the event had to be abandoned in 2020 and 2021. The festival stops well short of the archetypal 'rape and pillage' depiction of the Norsemen, who were far more domesticated than previously thought. However, hoards of fearsome-looking volunteer 'Vikings' dress up, stage a parade, and put on a mock battle before assembling on the headland looking out to sea.

Address Main Street, Heysham, LA3 2RN | Getting there By car, from M6 J34, follow the A683 to Heysham Village; bus 1A from Morecambe | Hours Mar–Oct, daily 10am–4pm, plus Sunday services | Tip Nearby St Peter's Church Hall, a converted stable building, is open 11am–3pm for events and exhibitions, and houses a welcoming café.

96 St Wilfrid's Church

Tolkien's Lord of the Rings *country*

It's hard to prove definitively, but the question being asked makes for fascinating conjecture: did J. R. R. Tolkien take the Hobbit name of 'Drogo' in his epic *Lord of the Rings* from a church notice board in old Lancashire? There, on a painted board inside the Medieval St Wilfrid's Parish Church in Ribchester, in the heart of the Ribble Valley, is a list of rectors dating from 1246 – the first of which is the single name, 'Drogo'.

It's perfectly possible that Tolkien took note as he hatched the characters and plots for his Middle Earth tale. After all, he wrote much of it while staying at Stonyhurst College, just a few miles away from St Wilfrid's (see ch. 93). Following the successful publication of *The Hobbit* during the 1930s, Tolkien concentrated on writing *Lord of the Rings*, moving into a gatehouse on the Stonyhurst estate with his wife and children. There, in a quiet classroom in the college itself, is where he wrote much of his fantasy masterpiece. Today, the great Oxford Professor of Anglo-Saxon and English Literature is honoured by the New Tolkien Library. This was opened in 2002 in the college's prep school, St Mary's Hall, where his son Michael once taught. In addition, in the surrounding great outdoors that Tolkien loved, a self-guided Tolkien Trail has been marked out. The 5.5-mile circular trail starts and ends at The Shireburn Arms in Hurst Green, a village close to Stonyhurst.

First off is a pathway to the banks of the fast-flowing River Ribble, turning east to walk upstream, before branching off up the River Hodder valley. Finally, take in the majesty of Stonyhurst College, which has been described as 'the finest Elizabethan house in the North'. Looking back, as you walk the length of the driveway past the two aligned lakes, it is a scene reminiscent of the grand stately home featured in *Brideshead Revisited*, and a magnificent view in every way.

LIST OF THE RECTORS OF RIBCHESTER

1243	BEFORE	DROGO.
1243		GUY DE ROUSILLON.
1246		IMBERTIUS.
1292		ROBERT DE POLKELINGTON.
1343		WALTER DE WOODHOUSE.
1343		WILLIAM DE WAKEFIELD.
1351		WILLIAM DE HORNBY.
1364		JOHN DE LINCOLN.
1367		LAMBERT DE THYRKYNGHAM.
1367		WILLIAM BOLTON.
1391-2		RICHARD DE WALLMESLEY.
1395		JOHN FARMER.
1414		JOHN DEL MORE.
1419		RICHARD COVENTRY.
1419		JOHN ELLYSWYK.
1466		ROBERT BROMLAW.
1476-7		WILLIAM TALBOT.
1505		ROBERT CROMBLEHOLME.
1527		WILLIAM CLAYTON.
1532		THOMAS THIRLEBY.
1542-3		GEORGE WOLFYTT.
1552		JAMES LIUNGARD.
1572		CHRISTOPHER ALSOP.
1573-4		HENRY NORCROSSE.
1616		RICHARD LEAROYDE.
1617-18		CHRISTOPHER HENDLEY.
1647		WILLIAM INGHAM.
1681		GEORGE OGDEN.
1706		THOMAS JOHNSON.
1738-9		JOHN HEBER.
1775		JOHN GRIFFITH.
1776		JOHN ATKINSON.
1798		ISAAC RELPH.
1801		JAMES QUARTLEY.
1829		BOULTBY THOMAS HASLEWOOD.
1876		FREDERICK EUGENE PERRIN.
1885		FRANCIS JOHN DICKSON.
1892		EVAN HARRIES.
1907		JOHN WILLIAM BROOKER.
1914		FRANK TITE.
1918		GEORGE MORGAN.
1924		SAMUEL SIDEBOTHAM.
1943		WILLIAM IRA BROWN.
1945		JOHN HALLIWELL FINCH.
1951		JOHN SHERARD BARNES WALLIS.
1970		EDWARD MAURICE JOHN CORNISH.
1978		ALAN JOHN CAVE.
1985		FRANK HEMSLEY LEVICK.
1991		ANDREW DAVID HINDLEY.

Address St Wilfrid's Church, Riverside, Ribchester, PR3 3XS | **Getting there** By car, M6 to J32, then B5269 and B6243 | **Tip** The Shireburn Arms, a fine gastropub and hotel in nearby Hurst Green, is named after Richard Shireburn, who helped build the college from the 16th century onwards (www.shireburnarmshotel.co.uk).

97 __ Sunderland Point of Entry

Lancashire's cotton trail began here

Little Sunderland Point may be a historic port whose time came and went, but it lays claim to a hugely-significant event that helped kick-start Britain's Industrial Revolution. It's said that the first bale of cotton ever to come to our shores from the New World was unloaded at Sunderland Point at the mouth of the River Lune. Ultimately, Manchester and further flung areas of Lancashire became the heartland of the cotton textile industry, fuelled by coal from the Lancashire mines. Sunderland faded away as Liverpool became the primary port for the American trade, with Manchester following suit when the Ship Canal opened up in the late 19th century.

However, no-one can take away Sunderland's hour of Old Glory. Today, its two rows of river-front warehouses, homes and quays bathe in the beauty of the tidal estuary, and the reflected glory of its magnificent seascapes. Long gone are the days when it was a bustling outport for Lancaster, which could not accommodate the larger vessels involved in the triangular trade between Britain, West Africa and North America. That was in the 18th century when Quaker businessman Robert Lawson launched the development of Sunderland Point. It was a blow when he went bankrupt in 1728, but the bigger blow was the building of Glasson Dock, which could service the import-export trade much better from across the Lune. With a canal link to Lancaster and Preston, and the subsequent railway connection to the West Coast Line, Sunderland was finished. It tried to re-invent itself as a spa resort – 'Little Brighton on the Lune' – but faded into the sleepy fishing, boating and artistic community it is today.

For almost 200 years a 'cotton tree' grew at Sunderland Point. The tree, said to be actually a cotton fluff-bearing kapok, fell during a fierce storm on New Year's Day, 1998, though a section of its trunk remains.

Address LA3 3HP | **Getting there** By car from Lancaster, head for the A 589 / Bay Gateway/A 683, turn left to Overton, then across the tidal road to Sunderland Point | **Hours** Check tide times: access at low tides only | **Tip** There are no cafés or pubs in Sunderland Point; the Ship Inn at nearby Overton is a traditional village pub, serving food and drink from noon daily.

98 Temperance Club

Abstinence makes the tea grow stronger

Ever wondered about the origin of the word 'teetotal'? It's all down to a stammer. Lancastrian Richard Turner, who started the movement to curb the results of alcohol consumption – drunkenness, gambling, debt and poverty – intended to call the movement 'totalism'. However, his stammer turned it into 'teetotalism', and the term stuck.

Lancaster and Morecambe had their fair share of teetotal premises, which practised complete abstinence, and temperance establishments, which prescribed moderation. On Morecambe Promenade, you can find the beautifully-curved glass frontage of the old Temperance Club, with those very words still inscribed above the entrance. The club was also a hotel, which had a restaurant and dining rooms for 'decent working men and women – people of good character'.

Keen support for the Temperance Club came from Morecambe's Methodist movement. Their chapels and churches were much in evidence, notably the Wesleyan Chapel on Green Street, the Free Methodist Chapel on Clarence Street and Trinity Methodist Church in the West End. They encouraged clubs and pubs to limit customers to two pints, encouraging landlords to refuse to serve drunks with any more alcohol. By the late 19th century, nearly three million people had signed 'the Pledge' nationwide. The Teetotalists even campaigned for the closing of pubs in outlying villages, such as Sunderland Point and Quernmore, issuing tokens which could be exchanged for non-alcoholic drinks.

However, over time, the movement was increasingly seen as opposing freedom of choice or being patronising, and support began to fade away, especially during the 20th century. It's ironic, but Morecambe's seafront premise is now the Temperance Club Barbers, offering a pint of draught lager or locally-brewed ale as well as a haircut, shave, beard trim, or even a shoe shine. A clear case of a 'trim and tonic'.

Address 240 Marine Road Central, Morecambe, LA4 4BJ | **Getting there** Six-minute walk from the Midland Hotel, along Marine Road Central, virtually opposite the Eric Morecambe Statue | **Hours** Public access on the Promenade | **Tip** Another blast from the past is Bayside Emporium, just along Marine Road Central on the seafront (LA4 4BQ). Their stock of antiques, furniture and collectibles spill out from the shopfront next to the pavement.

99 The Thankful Villages
Great Escape, at the double

The term 'Thankful Village', or 'Blessed Village', was popularised by writer Arthur Mee in his book *Enchanted Land* in 1936, and has special resonance to the north east of Lancaster. The chances of a village being left entirely unscathed by the First World War's human devastation are pretty remote. There were very few communities that saw all their menfolk return safely. In gratitude, those that did were called 'Thankful Villages' – and Lancashire has two of them.

Remarkably, and coincidentally, the two villages are just a few miles away from each other: Arkholme-with-Cawood and Nether Kellet – the latter being barely six miles from the centre of Lancaster. Nether Kellet even pulled off the same feat in the Second World War, becoming a 'Double Thankful Village' – something almost unheard of. Its status is quite astounding when considering the fact that only 53 villages out of the 16,000 in the whole of England and Wales defied the odds to gain 'thankful' status. Not one was identified in Scotland or Ireland, and for the Second World War, only 14 British villages saw all their members of the armed forces return.

Nether Kellet, with a current population of 663, sent 21 men to World War One, and 16 in the next conflagration. Arkholme, currently a hamlet of 333 people, sent 59 of its inhabitants in 1914, with each and every one returning. When you realise that more than 886,000 British were slaughtered in the wartime carnage, the double 'escape' in Lancashire is all the more astonishing. Today, a small peace memorial stands unceremoniously in Nether Kellett to remind visitors and locals of the lucky escape from the killing machine that caused such anguish for so many families and generations. Ironically, Arkholme has the remains of its own 'motte', a fortified mound, the Lune Valley having a large distribution of such early defensive works.

Address LA6 1DZ | Getting there By car, from junction 34 on the M6, take the Halton turn off the roundabout, follow Kirkby Lonsdale Road, and turn left to Nether Kellet; Arkholme is a 10-minute drive away | Tip The nearby village of Over Kellet is a rare example of having its village green dissected by a crossroads.

100 Thurnham Hall

Jacobite rebel pays a hefty price

Thurnham Hall may look peaceful enough in its tranquil rural setting just to the south west of Lancaster – but that serenity masks its turbulent religious past. This current-day resort and hotel, with its fine Jacobean Hall and Tudor fireplace, was the home of John Dalton, who sided with the Jacobites during the 1715 rebellion against the king.

Dalton, a staunch Catholic on the North Lancashire scene, joined James Edward Stuart's forces after they came down from Scotland to invade England, entering Lancaster in the late autumn of that fateful year. Dalton's open insurrection and his defiant Catholic stance put him on to a direct collision course with the powers-that-be, putting his life at risk. After releasing the religious prisoners in Lancaster Castle, the Catholic rebels marched south to Preston, where Dalton was taken prisoner, and sent off to London's Marshalsea Prison.

Seven months later, he was tried, found guilty of insurrection, and condemned to death. He appealed, and after a Protestant priest spoke up for him, he was pardoned and freed, to then walk the entire 200 miles from London to Lancaster. His seized estates were only returned after he paid a fine of £6000 – an immense fee more than 300 years ago.

The Grade I-listed hall has seen change and rebirth over the 800 years that it remained in the Thurnham family, from the 12th century until the passing of the last of the line in 1982. It has had its frontage altered and is now the epitome of a fine country house. In the majestic Great Hall, the focal point is the Tudor fireplace, with a Jacobean staircase, Elizabethan plasterwork on the ceiling, oak panelling and armorial windows. Like the Dalton family, who sided with the Royalists during the English Civil War, it is a survivor. It was touch and go during the Catholic persecution period of the 18th century, but the name lives on.

Address Thurnham Hall, Thurnham, LA2 0DT | Getting there Bus 89 to Knott End leaves Lancaster bus station every 90 minutes; by car, from the A6 near Lancaster Infirmary, take Ashton Road to the hall entrance on the A588 | Hours Daytime hotel hours | Tip It's worth visiting Lancaster's prestigious Dalton Square, which is named after the family, who owned the land as part of their estate; the square has several surviving Georgian houses, and Robert, son of rebel John, had a house there.

101 _Time and Tide_ Bell

Artwork that dropped a clanger

Both the time and the tide were running out for Morecambe's latest piece of ingenious artwork. A glitch looked set to sink the smooth launch of the _Time and Tide_ exhibit on Morecambe's Stone Jetty as it neared its grand opening day. The artwork was designed to make a bell react to the waves of Morecambe Bay as the tide rose up the side of the jetty. However, international artist Marcus Vergette realised there was a problem – and he had to work like the clappers to make the bell work. The initial clapper had fallen off, and a new and modified one had to be made, and quickly.

Apparently, the huge tidal range of Morecambe Bay had not been taken fully into account, and the modifications had to be made. In the end, any potential embarrassment was turned skilfully into the perfect, pre-launch publicity: the new clapper was fitted, and the grand opening of the moving piece of art took place. The bell, attached to the Stone Jetty, is designed to ring around high tide, and aims to remind the public of the rising sea levels caused by climate change. Played by the movement of the waves, the bell creates a varying pattern. As the sea level rises, the periods of bell strikes become more frequent, and as it submerges in the rising water the pitch will vary. For the public, it's all very technical, but very tuneful too.

Morecambe's _Time and Tide_ project has the backing of the Morecambe Artist Colony and is the latest of seven national projects spread across the United Kingdom, the first in Appledore, Devon, back in 2009. Now, bells have been placed in Bosta Beach on the Isle of Lewis in the Outer Hebrides; then on London's Trinity Buoy Wharf. Two Welsh locations followed, at Aberdovey and then Cernaes in Anglesey, with Lincolnshire's Mablethorpe next. But it was Morecambe that provided the last-minute drama, that final adjustment, and that invaluable, high-profile launch publicity.

Address Stone Jetty, Morecambe, LA4 4NJ | Getting there Behind the Midland Hotel on Marine Road | Hours Daytime, year-round | Tip Morecambe's beautifully-renovated Stone Jetty was once a working cargo and ferry terminal, complete with railway line that served passengers leaving for Ireland, the Isle of Man, and even Scotland. Today, its red tarmac surface, seabird sculptures and playful design offerings provide the perfect quay to the sea for strollers.

102 Trough of Bowland

Pass over Lancashire's Little Switzerland

It may not be the Swiss Alps' Brenner Pass, but the route between Lancaster and the Ribble Valley is high up there on Lancashire's tick list. The upland road pass through the wonderfully-named Trough of Bowland is pushing towards 1,000 feet, and has quite an elemental feel to it: not for nothing is the area known as Lancashire's 'Little Switzerland'! The pass is a scenic attraction in itself. It's a paradise and a challenge for both walkers and cyclists – and a majestic journey for car travellers too. En route, a scenic viewpoint above the hamlet of Quernmore lets you take in the whole coastal expanse of Morecambe Bay, with the Lake District hills and fells in the far distance, beyond the expanse of sandbars, river channels and the glistening seawater. Looking west, the sunsets are simply glorious.

At the head of the pass is the Old Grey Stone of Trough, marking the old border between Yorkshire and Lancashire, long before the City of Lancaster expanded its hinterland towards the slopes of the Pennine chain of hills and mountains. The old Forest of Bowland is in fact a specified Area of Outstanding Natural Beauty, and covers just over 300 square miles of land, which was deemed worthy of protection and conservation back in 1964. It incorporates parts of Greater Lancaster, the Ribble Valley, and Pendle – all in Lancashire – and Craven in North Yorkshire. It has a rugged beauty, with its gritstone hills, deep valleys and peat moorland: the names Grit Fell, Wolfhole Crag and Hell Crag speak for themselves.

Those with a historic interest will be fascinated to learn of its Viking past, with the western area becoming known as Amounderness after a leader who took control from the Northumbrian-based Vikings back in the 7th century. That was before it was axed and incorporated by the Anglo-Saxon's King Aethelstan in the 10th century.

Address Quernmore, LA2 9EH, and Dunsop Bridge, BB7 3BB | Getting there By car, from the A6 south in Lancaster, turn left into Moor Lane and Wyresdale Road, and on through Quernmore and over to Dunsop Bridge | Tip Jubilee Tower is a square stone structure on the summit of Quernmore Brow, and has breath-taking views over Morecambe Bay. It was built by Liverpool shipbuilder James Harrison to celebrate Queen Victoria's Diamond Jubilee.

103 Trowbarrow Quarry

Ta, Mac, for the limestone

The huge cliff faces of the defunct North Lancashire limestone quarries provide majestic backcloths for abundant wildlife sanctuaries. Yet behind these modern-day scenes of natural tranquillity lies a story of invention and ingenuity that helped transform the surface of everything that moves. The fusion of hot, crushed limestone and hot tar from Carnforth Gas Works created a tarmac-style product they called 'Quarrite' – and road surfaces were never the same again. Other road engineers were making tracks themselves, with John McAdam leading the way in Scotland. However, in Lancashire, Trowbarrow Quarry was the centre of this road-building revolution, even though the area's quarries started out making lime for building, industry and agriculture.

In their heyday, they were dirty, noisy and dangerous places, coating the surrounding trees and hedgerows with white dust. Once the technique for making quarrite was discovered, the cliff faces became bigger still, receiving a major boost when the Carnforth to Barrow railway line opened up in 1857, the tracks passing right by Trowbarrow. Remnants of the industry can still be seen in the quarry: the route of the inclined plane is evident, though the continuous-chain rail system that took limestone from the quarry face has long gone. By the railway could be found the crushing plant, the lime kiln, and the tarmac production building. One celebrated place to benefit from quarrite – billed as 'the new, dustless paving' – was Blackpool Promenade, which was one of the first places to see the material used.

Trowbarrow and Warton quarries were in production until the late 1950s, though tarmac production continued, using stone from the nearby Middlebarrow and Sandside quarries. The quarries are a climbers' Heaven, and a wildlife lovers' haven. Geologists love them too, as the Lower Carboniferous rocks are rich in fossils.

Address Trowbarrow Quarry Nature Reserve, Silverdale, LA5 0SS | **Getting there**
30-minute walk from Silverdale station and Leighton Moss RSPB on Storrs Lane; by car,
there's a small lay-by for parking on Storrs Lane, at the station or RSPB | **Hours** Mon–Sat
9am–5pm, Sun 9am–4pm | **Tip** Leighton Moss RSPB site has the largest reed bed in
North West England. Starling murmurations are spectacular just before dusk, and the avocet
and bittern have returned to breed.

104_ Victoria Wood's Café

One soup… and another soup

Victoria Wood is a legend in the world of comedy… all thanks to 'people watching' in Morecambe. For starters, her classic 'Two Soups' sketch, starring fellow comedienne Julie Walters, is said to be based on observing waitresses in one of the resort's old-fashioned cafés during the time she lived in Morecambe.

The waitress in the sketch is what is known as a 'nippy', the type who wore the traditional, maid-like black uniform, with white apron and matching white hat. It was the typical uniform of the J. Lyons tea rooms in London, and was worn in the old-style Lubin Café on Morecambe's seafront. The Lubin closed for business after the elderly ladies who ran it retired, though the sign is still there, with the name fading, but intact.

At the time, Victoria lived nearby, not far from the seafront, with her husband Geoff, and is known to have visited several Promenade cafés, along with her friend Julie Walters. Their observations inspired the famous soup sketch, with 'Old Mrs Cornthwaite' said to have provided much of the inspiration for the sketch. As with the TV character, she wasn't as fast on her feet as the archetypal 'nippy' waitresses in the J. Lyons tea rooms.

However, there was no malice in the sketch, though the humour was based on the slowness of the service, as well as the brilliant dialogue delivered by Walters, the inadvertent tipping of the soup from the bowls, and the sheer frustration of the waiting couple (Celia Imre and Duncan Preston) who had a train to catch. Add to all this, the fertile imagination and the comedienne's well-crafted script, and you have an absolute classic. Although, Victoria was from the Lancashire town of Bury, and lived in nearby Rossendale for a spell, she owed much to her time in Morecambe, as it was there that she fully developed her acts and scripts, before moving to north Lancashire.

Address 310 Marine Road Central, Morecambe, LA4 5AA | **Getting there** 11-minute walk north-east along Morecambe's Marine Road Central | **Hours** Always accessible | **Tip** There's no plaque, but from the pavement, you can see the upstairs flat where Victoria Wood lived at 12 Oxford Street, Morecambe, LA4 5JF.

105__ The View Café
Morecambe's blasts from the past

When you walk through the door of The View Café on Morecambe's seafront promenade, you realise that the old joke 'Nostalgia isn't what it used to be' doesn't play that well in this old resort. Nostalgia is certainly alive and well for those who love the sights and sounds of the Sixties. The 'View Café and Vintage Music' is a magnet for musicians, rock 'n roll devotees, and vintage record collectors from throughout the country – and a hearty meal or cup of coffee are also available into the bargain. Visitors can enjoy the view of Morecambe Bay in front, and a blast from the past behind.

The retro-themed offering was the idea of former guitarist and singer Peter Blackburn and his wife Marilyn. The couple were walking along the seafront, past the empty premises that what would become their future business place, when they saw the property owner changing the lock. They had a chat, and discovered that the previous tenant had decided to leave. Within days, Peter and Marilyn had opened up their vintage venture, with Peter giving up his market stall business selling records collected over the previous 60 years. These came in handy later, though, providing decor for the walls, place mats on the tables, and the stock for sales at bargain prices. The shop even has a set of newspapers reporting major musical events in the 1960s and 1970s.

The result is a colourful and quirky café-cum-shop, which has proven popular with the public, and brought a new way of life for the couple and their daughter Charlotte, who helps them in front of house. Thousands of albums and CDs are on sale, posters from rock concerts hang on the walls, alongside authentic electric guitars. Pete, now in his late seventies, can also look back on the days when he shared a stage with Johnny Cash, Kris Kristofferson, the Hollies, and Karl Denver, to name but a few, with many-a tale to tell. Canine friendly, and even a free sausage for your dog!

Address 281 Marine Road Central, Morecambe, LA4 5BY | **Getting there** Short drive or eight-minute walk from Morecambe railway station | **Hours** Tue–Sun 9.30am–4pm | **Tip** The seafront Clock Tower on Marine Road Central was built in 1905 in red brick with sandstone bands, and is quite a feature.

106_ V-sign Bridge

I swear that's its name

With suitable Lancastrian irreverence, Lancaster's Millennium Bridge for cyclists and pedestrians is called the V-sign Bridge. It appears to be putting two fingers up to the town, with its huge steel masts erected in such a way as to resemble the letter 'V'. In fact, it's been welcomed with open arms by the 3,000 people using the curved and aesthetically-appealing structure across the River Lune each day. At last, they could avoid the horrendous prospect of dicing with death on the one-way traffic Greyhound and Skirton Bridges, which are used by 20,000 vehicles a day.

Maybe the V-sign was aimed at the critics, who mainly came from the nearby riverside flats. They claimed it would be a white elephant, and tried to kill off the project. The figures tell a different story, however, with most people also appreciating the curved shape of the cable-held structure. It's been estimated that the number of cyclists and pedestrians crossing the river has increased by 16 per cent since the bridge was put in place. In most people's book, it's both safe, aesthetically pleasing and ecologically sound. It's certainly a vast improvement on the pedestrian way across the river downstream on the side of the Carlisle Bridge. This carries the main West Coast railway line, and has a long and tortuous flight of steps leading up to it.

Not that the Millennium Bridge project went as smoothly as a well-oiled bicycle. It missed the planned opening date of the Festival of Cycling in June, 2000, then the Cyclefest in August. One major technical problem came with lifting the giant masts, when the four-day booking of a 1,000-ton crane turned into five weeks. Then one of the sub-contractors went bust. In the end, the bridge finally opened in 2001. Even then, the opening ceremony couldn't be done by Lancaster's famous cyclist Jason Queally, who crashed out the day before – literally!

Address LA1 1AY | Getting there Five-minute walk from Lancaster bus station; by car, pass through Lancaster on the A 6, turn left on Damside, then park on St George's Quay | Hours Always accessible | Tip Along the riverbank, downstream from the bridge, is a row of five-storey, 18th-century warehouses that afford a characterful sight alongside the old Customs House, now Lancaster Maritime Museum; many of the warehouses are now modern apartments, with two ancient pubs still operating below.

107 War Memorial Village

All quiet on the Westfield front

A poignant letter from a soldier in the Great War had a significant effect back home in Lancaster. This correspondence triggered the young man's father to do something for the injured and shell-shocked victims and their families; and the village that he built for them is still there to this day.

Westfield Memorial Village, just down the hill from Lancaster Railway Station, was the idea of local architect and landscape designer Thomas Mawson: it was his son James who wrote the letter before being killed in action himself. Initially, 31 cottages were built on land donated by Herbert Storey, son of former Mayor and local MP Sir Thomas Storey. Public and individual subscriptions funded the charitable scheme, and eventually many more homes were built, with priority given to those who had suffered – a principle that is maintained to this day. Mawson stipulated that each home should have a garden – for therapy, pride and a feeling of well-being. The streets are tree-lined, and a central roundabout has on it a statue of a soldier handing a drink of water to a wounded colleague. British Army top brass, including Field Marshal Douglas Haig, came to the official opening in 1924, but there is no glorification of war, just the depiction of a helping hand.

Mawson's initial idea was for small workplaces to be provided, giving residents the opportunity to practise their pre-war trades and show off their handiwork. However, opposition from local businesses and trade unions killed off this idea. More long-lasting was the bowling green and social club that were part of the village. Fund raising still continues for maintenance work, though in 1987 the village was leased to a housing association for finance to modernise the houses. The village is a lasting legacy to Thomas Mawson, a boy born into relative poverty in Nether Wyresdale, but a man who left his mark.

Address 30 West Road, Lancaster, LA1 5QG | Getting there By car, two minutes from Lancaster railway station, along West Road, then into Storey Avenue. Six minutes by foot. | Hours Mon–Fri 8am–4pm | Tip Lancaster's International War Museum Memorial, a winged figure of peace, is adjacent to Lancaster City Hall in Dalton Square.

108 West End Gardens Frame

Picture-perfect seaside scene in Morecambe

It's often said: 'If you're going to do something, do it properly.' You might also add: 'Do it big, and do it boldly.' This old adage was never more apt than in the commissioning of a public art display to be sited in Morecambe's West End Gardens. Local schoolchildren were asked for their input, and the result was a series of large, showpiece artefacts, including a giant picture frame. The five- by three-metre timber structure does not have a canvas, and it's therefore possible to look through it from either side. Seawards, it frames the beauty of Morecambe Bay and the distant Lakeland hills; landwards, it puts the row of traditional, seafront B&B hotels well and truly in the picture.

The project aimed to reflect the theme of the four elements: earth, wind, water and fire. Given the dramatic sunsets in Morecambe Bay, the sun was chosen to reflect the concept of heat, and perhaps a little abstrusely, the idea of fire. The edge of the giant picture frame has rebated ceramic tiles, which illustrate the full range of colours witnessed during a sunset. To take it all in, passers-by can even sit on the frame.

The concept of wind was depicted by seven stainless steel trumpets bunched together, with wires inside to catch the wind and disperse the sound. The display is four metres tall, though each trumpet is different in shape, size and direction, thereby sounding out in all directions. The idea of earth is exemplified by a three-metre bench of six, different glacial rocks found in the local area. The large rocks have been split in half, then polished and set in Corten steel, making an enticing place for promenaders to sit. Finally, the idea of water is illustrated by the concept of Morecambe Bay tides. A cast-iron dome represents the earth, with smaller domes representing the cycle of the moon, whose gravitational pull causes the tides.

Address Marine Road West, West End, Morecambe, LA3 1BY | Getting there A short drive or a 15-minute walk from Morecambe station | Tip Nearby is The Beach Café, a stylish, glass-sided venue which offers good food, friendly service, and panoramic views across the bay.

109 The White Bull
'Cheers' to Roman pillars of the community

The White Bull is a classic name for a rural pub, though not many have a classical entrance dating back to Roman times. The stone pillars on either side of the doorway into Ribchester's 18th-century hostelry in Lancashire's Ribble Valley are said to have come from the hamlet's Roman fort, dating back to around 100 AD. If you go through the pub and restaurant into the beer garden at the back, you can sip your drink and look out over the ancient remains of the Roman Bathhouse.

Apparently, the pillars were found in the nearby River Ribble, which was a fording point on the Roman road that was a continuation of Watling Street. The straight-as-a-die road ran from Dover to London, on to St Albans, and then to Wroxeter, near Shrewsbury, and beyond. Little 'Rib', as it is known locally, was an important crossroads on the Roman road north from the fort in what is now the city of Manchester. One route from Rib went west to Galgate, then north through Lancaster and on to Cumbria.

The original name of Ribchester fort is a bit of a tongue-twister: Bremetennacum. It was built to guard the river crossing point, and keep the locals under control. As you stroll around the exposed remains, your mind flashes back to 72 AD, when the first timber and earth structure was put in place. That was at a time when Emperor Verpassian ruled the roost, and when Agricola was governor. Around 100 AD, a stone structure was built, with around 500 foreign conscripts from Spain being drafted in for duty at Ribchester, followed by a second unit brought in from Hungary. The granary, exposed in St Wilfrid's churchyard, and the bathhouse, can still be seen, and the excellent Ribchester Roman Museum tells you the whole story. The museum was founded in 1915 by Margaret Greenall, a member of the famous brewing family, so raise a glass to her when you visit The White Bull.

Address Church Street, Ribchester, PR3 3XP, +44 (0)1254 878048,
www.whitebullribchester.com | Getting there By car, M6 south to J32; under five miles
from Stonyhurst College | Hours Wed, Thu, Sun noon–11pm, Fri & Sat noon–midnight |
Tip Head to the Ribble Way path alongside the river, heading upstream, either all the way
to Clitheroe, or just part of the tranquil, 11-mile walk from Ribchester.

110_ Winning Post Church

Racehorse victory makes Holy history in Dunsop

It's not every day that a church is built from the proceeds of a win at the races. But if you have the prize money and the proceeds from a bet after your horse unexpectedly wins the 1861 Derby, you can afford to get across the line in the religious stakes. That's the story behind the building of St Hubert's RC Church just outside Dunsop Bridge in the Ribble Valley, on the road leading to the Trough of Bowland pass and on to Lancaster.

The horse was called Kettledrum, and was owned by Colonel Charles Towneley. He lived at nearby Thoneyholme Hall, and his private family chapel was used by fellow Catholics in the Hodder Valley, as they had no local church. In the race itself, Kettledrum was being beaten by the favourite, Dundee, who was easily ahead at Tattenham Corner. With only eight yards to go to the winning post, however, the horse broke down, letting Kettledrum come through to win by a neck. Not that Kettledrum was a novice. During the 12 months between August, 1860 and September, 1861, he ran eight times and won four races, also finishing second in the 2000 Guineas and St Leger.

What's equally remarkable is that this small country church is the work of Catholic convert Edward Pugin, son of the architect Augustus Welby Pugin, who was chosen as the interior designer of the Palace of Westminster for its reconstruction following the 1834 fire. Edward concentrated on churches, and is perhaps best-known for his design of the majestic Gorton Monastery in Manchester.

The interior of St Hubert's is quite a spectacle, with a medieval font, painted decorations and beautiful windows, made by one of the greatest stained-glass practitioners of the day: Jean Baptiste Carpronnier, of Brussels. On the side pillars of the altar are four small carvings of a horse's head, and on the wall is a painting of a racehorse – Kettledrum, of course.

Address Trough End, Dunsop Bridge, BB7 3BG, +44 (0)200 423307, www.olotv.org.uk |
Getting there By car, 15 miles from Lancaster, via Wyresdale Road and the Trough of
Bowland pass; bus 51 from Clitheroe Railway Station runs every couple of hours | Hours
See website for current information on visiting | Tip There are some challenging walks
nearby, including Salter Fell Track – a tough pass along which the Pendle witches were
taken for trial at Lancaster Castle in 1612.

111__Winter Gardens

Where mill girls could be duchesses for the day

The opulence, the style, the grandeur is still there to be seen. Morecambe's truly amazing, Grade II-listed 'People's Palace', as the old Winter Gardens was known, still enthrals. And if plans come to fruition, one of the grandest theatres in the entire country will soon be presenting spectacular offerings on stage. Before its closure in 1977, the Winter Gardens on Morecambe's sea front saw up to 3,000 fans a time come to see a huge array of top artists, such as Shirley Bassey, the Rolling Stones, The Shadows, Billy Connolly, The Who, Adam Faith, The Walker Brothers, and the Small Faces. Elgar and the Halle Orchestra have also played here, as have Laurel and Hardy.

When not undergoing major renovation work, the Winter Gardens is open to the public for booked tours on Saturdays and Sundays. The excitement at visiting what has been referred to as 'the Albert Hall of the North' remains undimmed. It is visually spectacular, from its beautifully-crafted balustrades to its stained-glass windows, from velvet seats in the dress circle to the more rough and ready seating 'in the Gods'. The beautiful, curved plaster ceiling – the largest expanse of fibrous plaster ceiling in the country – has been painstakingly restored by top craftsman, thanks to a generous grant from Historic England, and the hard work of the voluntary Winter Gardens Preservation Trust, which saved the building from any threat from the wrecker's hammer. They made sure it was seen as a national, not just a local, treasure.

Naturally, of course, the theatre is haunted, and is even said to have a good side and an evil side. One ghost is said to be a seamstress who never achieved her dream of becoming a dancer. Watch out in the dressing rooms! There are reports of ghostly happenings in the auditorium, stairwells and bar, with people claiming to be poked, prodded and pushed by mysterious presences.

Address 209 Marine Road, Morecambe, LA4 4BU | Getting there By car, once on the seafront from Central Drive, turn right at the roundabout near the Midland Hotel | Hours Sat & Sun 11am–4pm for booked tours | Tip Historical walks are on offer by local historian Peter Wade, who has 20 years' experience. From his 'Time Tour' to 'Art Deco', from 'Tap Rooms and Temperance Halls' to 'The Train now Standing' (www.exploremorecambebay.org.uk).

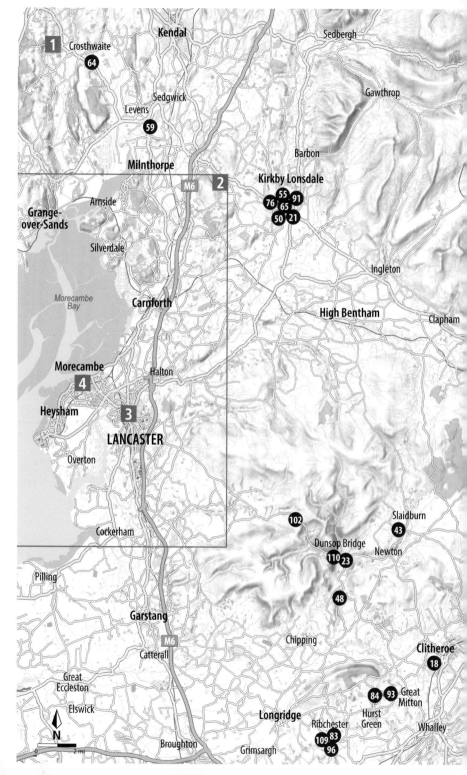

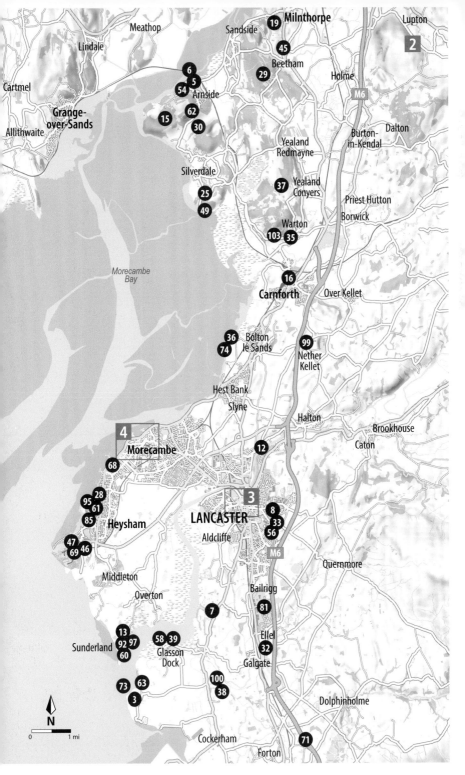

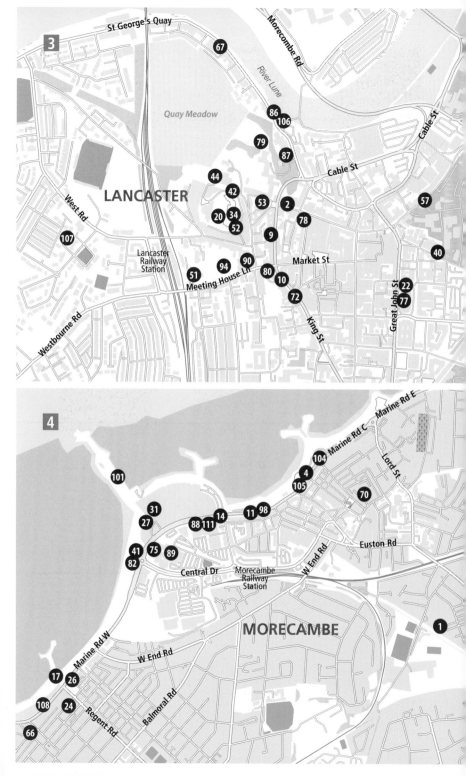

Ed Glinert, David Taylor
111 Places in Yorkshire
That You Shouldn't Miss
ISBN 978-3-7408-1167-9

David Taylor
111 Places in Newcastle
That You Shouldn't Miss
ISBN 978-3-7408-1043-6

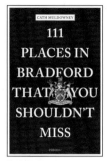

Cath Muldowney
111 Places in Bradford
That You Shouldn't Miss
ISBN 978-3-7408-1427-4

Kim Revill, Alesh Compton
111 Places in Leeds
That You Shouldn't Miss
ISBN 978-3-7408-0754-2

Michael Glover,
Richard Anderson
111 Places in Sheffield
That You Shouldn't Miss
ISBN 978-3-7408-0022-2

Julian Treuherz,
Peter de Figueiredo
111 Places in Manchester
That You Shouldn't Miss
ISBN 978-3-7408-0753-5

Julian Treuherz,
Peter de Figueiredo
111 Places in Liverpool
That You Shouldn't Miss
ISBN 978-3-7408-1607-0

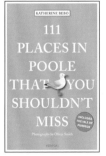

Katherine Bebo, Oliver Smith
111 Places in Poole
That You Shouldn't Miss
ISBN 978-3-7408-0598-2

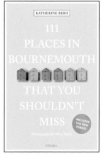

Katherine Bebo, Oliver Smith
111 Places in Bournemouth
That You Shouldn't Miss
ISBN 978-3-7408- 1166-2

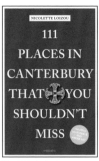

Nicolette Loizou
111 Places in Canterbury
That You Shouldn't Miss
ISBN 978-3-7408-0899-0

Philip R. Stone
111 Dark Places in England
That You Shouldn't Miss
ISBN 978-3-7408-0900-3

John Sykes, Birgit Weber
111 Places in London
That You Shouldn't Miss
ISBN 978-3-7408-1168-6

Ed Glinert, Marc Zakian
111 Places in London's
East End
That You Shouldn't Miss
ISBN 978-3-7408-0752-8

Solange Berchemin,
Martin Dunford, Karin Tearle
111 Places in Greenwich
That You Shouldn't Miss
ISBN 978-3-7408-1107-5

Nicola Perry, Daniel Reiter
33 Walks in London
That You Shouldn't Miss
ISBN 978-3-95451-886-9

Kirstin von Glasow
111 Gardens in London
That You Shouldn't Miss
ISBN 978-3-7408-0143-4

Laura Richards, Jamie Newson
111 London Pubs and Bars
That You Shouldn't Miss
ISBN 978-3-7408-0893-8

Emma Rose Barber,
Benedict Flett
111 Churches in London
That You Shouldn't Miss
ISBN 978-3-7408-0901-0

Solange Berchemin
**111 Places in the Lake District
That You Shouldn't Miss**
ISBN 978-3-7408-0378-0

Rob Ganley, Ian Williams
**111 Places in Coventry
That You Shouldn't Miss**
ISBN 978-3-7408-1044-3

Martin Booth, Barbara Evripidou
**111 Places in Bristol
That You Shouldn't Miss**
ISBN 978-3-7408-1612-4

Alexandra Loske
**111 Places in Brighton and
Lewes That You Shouldn't Miss**
ISBN 978-3-7408-0255-4

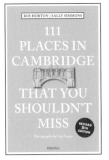

Rosalind Horton, Sally Simmons,
Guy Snape
**111 Places in Cambridge
That You Shouldn't Miss**
ISBN 978-3-7408-0147-2

Justin Postlethwaite
**111 Places in Bath
That You Shouldn't Miss**
ISBN 978-3-7408-0146-5

Gillian Tait
**111 Places in Edinburgh
That You Shouldn't Miss**
ISBN 978-3-95451-883-8

Tom Shields, Gillian Tait
**111 Places in Glasgow
That You Shouldn't Miss**
ISBN 978-3-7408-1488-5

Gillian Tait
**111 Places in Fife
That You Shouldn't Miss**
ISBN 978-3-7408-0597-5

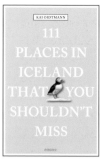

Kai Oidtmann
111 Places in Iceland
That You Shouldn't Miss
ISBN 978-3-7408-0030-7

Andrea Livnat,
Angelika Baumgartner
111 Places in Tel Aviv
That You Shouldn't Miss
ISBN 978-3-7408-0263-9

Sybil Canac, Renée Grimaud,
Katia Thomas
111 Places in Paris
That You Shouldn't Miss
ISBN 978-3-7408-0159-5

Thomas Fuchs
111 Places in Amsterdam
That You Shouldn't Miss
ISBN 978-3-7408-0023-9

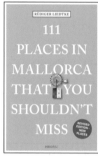

Rüdiger Liedtke
111 Places in Mallorca
That You Shouldn't Miss
ISBN : 978-3-7408-1049-8

Alexia Amvrazi,
Diana Farr Louis, Diane Shugart,
Yannis Varouhakis
111 Places in Athens
That You Shouldn't Miss
ISBN 978-3-7408-0377-3

Christine Izeki, Björn Neumann
111 Places in Tokyo
That You Shouldn't Miss
ISBN 978-3-7408-1277-5

Christoph Hein, Sabine Hein
111 Places in Singapore
That You Shouldn't Miss
ISBN 978-3-7408-0382-7

Jo-Anne Elikann
111 Places in New York
That You Must Not Miss
ISBN 978-3-95451-052-8

The key figures in making this book happen are Alistair Layzell and Laura Olk, providing invaluable amounts of help and guidance; photographer David Taylor, bringing his advice and invaluable experience; and perhaps most of all, my friend and fellow author Ed Glinert, who introduced me to the *111 Places* series, and who steered me through the creative process. A special thank you goes to local historian and guide Peter Wade, and to editor Martin Sketchley, who showed great forbearance. My deep gratitude goes to the late Cedric Robinson, Queen's Guide to the Morecambe Bay Sands, and to his lovely wife Olive. Cedric introduced me to the cross-bay walks and the joys of the area. So much so, that I became one of his assistants, and continue helping to take charity walks across the Kent Estuary from Arnside to Grange. Then there are the myriad of acknowledgements, ranging from Visit Lancashire, Visit Cumbria, Visit Lancaster, and Explore Morecambe Bay; to the staff at attractions and businesses; and to members of organisations throughout the localities. Above all, I am grateful to my wife 'Miss Mo', who has endured and enjoyed my preoccupations and trips in equal measure.
Lindsay Sutton

I couldn't have completed the photography for this book without the cheerful assistance of a good number of people. For their invaluable help I'd like to thank Jane Wignall at Beach Bird, Bob Warrior at the Royal King Arm's Hotel, Paolo at Brucciani's, Jane Meaker at Levens Hall, Helen and Malcolm O'Neil at the Winter Gardens Theatre, Canon Brian McConkey of St Wilfred's Church in Ribchester, Suzie Reynolds of Leighton Hall, Frazer at the Lancaster Maritime Museum, Aaron Williams at the Lancaster Golf Club, Mandy McKnight at the Grand Theatre, James Craig at Lancaster Brewery, Jimmy Blackburn at GB Antiques Centre, Bea, deputy warden of the Quaker Meeting House in Lancaster, Meridon Read at Soul Bowl, Valerie Laycock at The Jigsaw Lounge, and Ian Steel, Tom Mellors and the staff at Atkinsons Coffee Roasters. A huge thank you also to my wife Tania, who was there waiting whenever I came home from a trip to Lancashire.
David Taylor

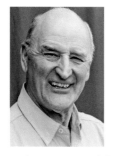

Lindsay Sutton was born in Yorkshire, but has lived in Lancashire for most of his life, beginning his journalist career in the Red Rose county. He has worked on the *Mirror*, the *Mail* and *The Times*, serving on both the domestic and international front. He has also worked for ITV, Sky and the BBC as a TV reporter and producer, and has notched up three lifetime writing awards, including IPW American Travel Writer of the Year. However, his heart remains set in the North of England. Significantly, his previous book, *Sands of Time*, was focussed on Morecambe Bay, tracking the former Queen's Guide Cedric Robinson: he remains an assistant on the charity-based walks across the bay.

David Taylor is a professional freelance landscape photographer and writer who lives in Northumberland. His first camera was a Kodak Instamatic. Since then he's used every type of camera imaginable: from bulky 4x5 film cameras to pocket-sized digital compacts. David has written nearly 40 books about photography, as well as supplying images and articles to both regional and national magazines. His first book for Emons was *111 Places in Newcastle That You Shouldn't Miss*. When David is isn't outdoors he can be found at home with his wife, a cat and a worryingly large number of tripods.